COMMUNICATION MODELS

COMMUNICATION MODELS

for the study of mass communications

DENIS MCQUAIL
and
SVEN WINDAHL

Longman
London and New York

Longman Group UK Limited
Longman House
Burnt Mill, Harlow, Essex CM20 2JE, England
and Associated Companies throughout the world

Published in the United States of America
by Longman Inc., New York

First published 1981
Second impression 1984
Third impression 1986
Fourth impression 1986
Fifth impression 1987

British Library Cataloguing in Publication Data
McQuail, Denis
Communication models for the study of mass communication.
1. Mass media – Research
I. Title II. Windahl, Sven
302.2'3 P91.3 80-41780
ISBN 0-582-29572-6

Produced by Longman Singapore Publishers Pte Ltd
Printed in Singapore

CONTENTS

1 INTRODUCTION

1.1 SCOPE AND PURPOSE

This book has a dual objective. On the one hand, it seeks to assemble and present, in a succinct and accessible form, many of the models which have been developed to describe or explain the communication, and in particular the mass communication, process. On the other hand, it aims to represent the main lines of thought about the process of mass communication which have emerged during the last 30 years of research into mass communication. It is thus a form of historical review, although we have included no model for purely historical reasons. While we cannot hope to provide a complete historical record of the field of study in this particular form, our wish to show at least the most important developments has led us at certain points to draw our own models which reflect important conceptual developments or relatively new fields of enquiry.

There is more than one way of telling the history of ideas about mass communication and the one we have chosen follows a tradition in which mass communication can be seen as a specific form of a general phenomenon, in which the main elements of sender, message and receiver take on distinctive characteristics and meanings. We hope to shed light on these meanings by starting with some very simplified and general versions of what any communication relationship involves and then proceeding to deal with the effects of mass communication and with the relationships which hold amongst the main participants and between the participants and their society.

In focussing on mass communication, we have inevitably to neglect interesting developments in the study of inter- and intra-personal communication and of communication structures and flows within groups and organizations. Nevertheless, our own view of mass communication is of a process which is co-extensive and interactive with other types of communication network and process. While different specialisms have emerged in the study of communication which seem to have little in common by the way of theory, method or aim, we would prefer not to mark clear boundaries around the substance of any one 'communication system'. We anticipate a future in which existing boundaries will become even less clear than they are at present and when communication technology and new expressions of communication need will produce different structures, relationships and possibilities of effect.

The activity of making communication models does not in general command a great deal of attention amongst students of mass communication at the present time. In the light of this, it might be asked why we should choose to swim against the tide. We point to general advantages and disadvantages in the following passages, but our main answer is that we are convinced of the heuristic value of the model. For us there is no inconsistency between an emphasis on substantive empirical research and the wish to formulate hypotheses, conclusions and theory in diagrammatic form.

1.2 THE USES AND MISUSES OF MODELS

For our purpose, we consider a model as a consciously simplified description in graphic form of a piece or reality. A model seeks to show the main elements of any structure or process and the relationships between these elements. Deutsch (1966) notes the following main advantages of models in the social sciences. Firstly, they have an *organizing function* by ordering and relating systems to each other and by providing us with images of wholes that we might not otherwise perceive. An aspect of this is that a model gives a *general* picture of a range of different particular circumstances. Secondly, they help in *explaining,* by providing in a simplified way information which would otherwise be complicated or ambiguous. This gives the model a *heuristic function*, since it can guide the student or researcher to key points of a process or system. Thirdly, the model may make it possible to *predict* outcomes or the course of events. It can at least be a basis for assigning probabilities to various alternative outcomes, and hence for formulating hypotheses in research. Some models claim only to describe the structure of a phenomenon. In this sense, a diagram of the components of a radio set could be described as 'structural'. Other models, which we call 'functional', describe systems in terms of energy, forces and their direction, the relations between parts and the influence of one part on another.

The models presented in this book fall mainly into the latter category, simply because all communication is in some degree dynamic and involves some elements of process or change. Even so, some of the models are very simple and tell us little about the forces at work which relate elements to each other. While models in general can be purely verbal, or diagrammatic, or mathematical, we have presented only those which are both verbal and diagrammatic.

It has been argued against the use of models that they tend to trap their originators and users within rather limited confines which they then become eager to defend against attack. Such a tendency can have a delaying effect on the development of a science, although this has probably not happened in the case of communication research, where old models have tended to be soon discarded or modified. A similar risk is that a model, or even a succession of models, can tend to perpetuate some initial questionable, but fundamental, assumptions about the components of a model or the processes at work. An example in the field of communication is the tendency to represent communication as a one-directional process in which a 'sender' deliberately tries to influence a 'receiver'. Such a representation tends to deny the circularity, negotiability and openness of much communication.

It should at least be remembered that there are some risks in using models, even for heuristic purposes. They are inevitably incomplete, oversimplified and involve some concealed assumptions. There is certainly no model that is suitable for all purposes and all levels of analysis and it is important to choose the correct model for the purpose one has in mind. One of the purposes of the book is to give some indication of the proper purpose and level of different models, partly by showing how they have been used in communication research. The reader should become aware of the possibilities of testing models against circumstances or cases and of adapting any given model to suit the chosen application. The models presented are not so sacred that they can not easily be given a somewhat different shape and formulation. It should become apparent that anyone is in a position to construct his own models of a given aspect of the communication process and we hope that this book will encourage students of mass communication to adopt this process as a means of elucidation.

We view models primarily as aids to thought which are especially appropriate in the study of communication. Why they should be so appropriate is not easy to demonstrate, but it may stem from the fact that communication is a binding force in social relationships without at the same time being visible or having tangible and permanent forms. Acts of communication take predictable or recurrent forms within a given structure of relationships and have consequences for this structure without being readily open to observation. There is, consequently, an attraction in being able to 'draw' the 'lines' which stand for the links we know to exist but cannot see and to use other devices to show the structure, topography, strength and direction of relationships. So much of the subject of communication has to be dealt with in verbal abstractions that it is an aid and a relief to have at least something 'fixed' in graphic form, however much the element of abstraction may remain.

1.3 DEFINITIONS AND TERMS

The central concept in this book is communication. It has been defined in a number of ways, but we do not wish or need to be tied to one particular definition, since the authors we refer to have different notions of the concept. But the following examples give us some idea of the variety of meanings involved:

The transmission of information, ideas, attitudes, or emotion from one person or group to another (or others) primarily through symbols (Theodorson and Theodorson 1969)

In the most general sense, we have communication wherever one system, a source, influences another, the destination, by manipulation of alternative symbols, which can be transmitted over the channel connecting them (Osgood et al. 1957)

Communication may be defined as 'social interaction through messages' (Gerbner 1967)

Thus, in the most general terms, communication implies a sender, a channel, a message, a receiver, a relationship between sender and receiver, an effect, a context in which communication occurs and a range of things to which 'messages' refer. Sometimes, but not always, there is an intention, or purpose to 'communicate' or to 'receive'. Communication can be any or all of the following: an *action on* others; an *interaction with* others and a *reaction to* others.

Sometimes the originators of models point to two additional processes, that of 'encoding' (at the sender end of the model) and that of 'decoding' (at the receiver end). Encoding means that the message is translated into a language or code suitable for the means of transmission and the intended receivers.

Decoding refers to the re-translation of the message in order to extract meaning. In a conversation between two persons, the encoding function is performed by the speech mechanism and (for non-verbal communication) muscles making possible getures, etc. In such a case, the senses of hearing and sight perform the decoding function. In mass communication encoding can refer to technical tranformations necessary for the transmission of signals and also to the systematic choice of words, pictures and formats according to established procedures and the expectations held about audience experience.

In many models, the concept of 'feedback' is employed. In general, this refers to any process by which the communicator obtains information as to whether and how his intended receiver has indeed received the message. Such information can help to modify ongoing or future communication behaviour. In a face to face communication situation this may take the form of questions, requests to repeat something, gestures, responses and so on. In mass communication, feedback of these kinds is mainly replaced by: audience research; sales figures; studio audiences; tryouts; letters and phone calls. But it can also take the form of response directly from superiors, colleagues, friends and other personal contacts.

As we have seen, many of the basic terms in communication take different meanings when they refer to mass communication and we need to have a different characterization of the latter. A frequently cited definition is as follows:

> Mass communications comprise the institutions and techniques by which specialized groups employ technological devices (press, radio, films, etc.) to disseminate symbolic content to large, heterogeneous and widely dispersed audiences (Janowitz 1968)

This points to most of the variations and additions that we need to take account of. The 'sender' in mass communication is always part of an organized group and often a member of an institution which has functions other than communication. The 'receiver' is always an individual but may often be seen by the sending organization as a group or collectivity with certain general attributes. The channel no longer consists of the social relationship, means of expression and sensory organs, but includes large scale technologically-based distribution devices and systems. These systems still have a social component, since they depend on law, custom and expectation. The message in mass communication is not a unique and transitory phenomenon, but a mass produced and infinitely repeatable symbolic structure, often of great complexity.

Of particular significance in mass communication are: the public and open nature of all communication; the limited and controlled access to 'sending' facilities; the impersonality of the relationship between sender and receiver; the imbalance of the relationship between them; the intervention of institutionalized arrangements between sender and receiver. In reality, there is no single universal form of the mass communication process and the diversity of the reality accounts in part for the multiplicity of possible models to represent the whole or parts of it.

1.4 EARLY COMMUNICATION MODELS AND MASS COMMUNICATION RESEARCH

Mass communication research, stimulated primarily by concern over the political influence of the mass press and later over the moral and social consequences of film and radio, extends back at least until the beginning of the present century. Research into communication in general had its origins in the wish to test and increase efficiency and effectiveness in the spheres of education, propaganda, telecommunication, advertising and public and human relations. Research activity began with practical concerns and was fed by developments in psychology and sociology and by general advances in methodology, especially the use of experiments, social surveys and statistics.

It was not really until after the Second World War that a focus on communication as such was articulated. Just as much early empirical research was largely an American phenomenon, so was it in the United States in the post-war period that the possibility of a science of communication was first discussed. The decade of the 1950s proved to be fertile in model-building activity, which can be taken as an expression of the search for growth and unity in the study of communication. According to Johnson and Klare (1961), it was a mathematician, Claude Shannon, who first provided the stimulus to social scientists to formulate their thinking about communication in model form according to the terms outlined above. The initial appeal of this approach can probably be related, first of all, to the predominance of the current interest in effects and effectiveness, secondly to its consistency with the stimulus-response model of behaviour control and learning which was fundamental to psychology (see 3.1 below) and thirdly, to the growing wish to order and codify existing knowledge and enquiry in mass communication research.

1.5 ELABORATION OF THE BASIC MATHEMATICAL MODEL

The simple sender-channel-message-receiver model was rapidly modified during the 1950s according to the interests both of the students of interpersonal communication and of mass communication. The changes took account of several important aspects of human communication. One was the need to incorporate more fully and as an essential component, the occurrence of feedback. Associated with this is the recognition of the non-linearity of communication processes. They are typically circular, recurrent and spiralling, since the change brought about by communication initiates a new 'loop' at a different point and on a different plane (to use spatial analogies) than at the start. These are discussed in 2.2 below, in connection with the work of Osgood, Schramm and Dance.

A second major development is related to the fact that receivers normally selectively perceive, interpret and retain messages. The potential inefficiency of a communication link was, of course, recognized in the earlier mathematical model, but the problem is there treated as 'noise' in the system, since the main criteria of successful communication are derived from the intentions of the sender. Gerbner's model (2.3) incorporates a solution to the problem which recognizes the substantive interest of the sources and nature of apparent inefficiency. He stresses the essentially *transactional* character of much communication and the dependence of any meaning which is acquired on the assumptions and fore-knowledge of the receiver and on the context in which communication takes place. One might sum up this development as having to do with the intersubjectivity of communication, since all communication involves more or less elaborate exchange and bargaining between senders and receivers. The result of communication is thus a matter of negotiation and cannot always be predicted in advance. This thought has continued to be important in recent work on interpersonal communication and has influenced the development of what we have labelled 'audience-centred' approaches to mass communication (Ch. 5).

1.6 FROM COMMUNICATION TO MASS COMMUNICATION

An obvious point of departure in the model-making tradition was the separation out of models concerned expressly with mass communication. It was essential to make specific allowance for the distinctive features of mass communication which have been briefly described. Thus, Schramm's adaptation of his own more general model recognized the collective nature of the sender and the social organization of the audience (2.6) and Riley and Riley (2.7) put particular emphasis on the formal and informal social settings which influence both sender and receiver and the relationship between them.

Maletzke (2.8) drew an elaborate model incorporating these and other ideas, especially those to do with variations between different media and types of content and the perceptions of each other which are formed by mass communicators and audiences. The work of Westley and MacLean (2.5) was especially important in emphasizing the role played by mass communication organizations in mediating and controlling the channels between sources in society and the general public. Their model also bridges the gap between the original basic model with its emphasis on purposive communication and the apparently purposeless flow of mass communication, in the sense of being continuous and not directed to known or specified receivers. In their model, the mass communicator acts as an agent for the receiver, an interpreter of needs and interests. Audience demand becomes a partial substitute for communicator purpose according to this view.

During the decades of the 1960s and 1970s, the focus of interest in research and relevant model-making has tended to move away from the search for a general understanding of the whole mass communication process and towards research on specific aspects of this process: longer-term social, cultural and ideological effects; the media organization and its relationship to society and audience; the social and psychological bases of audience choice and response; the structuring of typical content forms, especially news and 'reality' information. These subjects are dealt with in the relevant sections below, but certain broad developments in thinking and research can be summarized in advance.

1.7 DEVELOPMENTS IN COMMUNICATION MODELS AND COMMUNICATION RESEARCH

One important advance in thinking about the effects of mass communication had already been made before the sequence of models presented in this book had begun. The shift in question, recorded in our discussion of the 'two-step flow' of communication (3.3), was a move away from a conception of direct and blanket effects on a mass or aggregate audience and towards a recognition of the mediating part played by personal contacts in relaying and validating media-originated information and ideas. Underlying this shift is a decline in the currency of early mass society theories, which conceived the citizens of modern societies as vulnerable to manipulative uses of the media by power-holding élites.

A second development, of more recent origin, has been a change in the balance of interest from direct short-term effects (of the kind dealt with by Comstock in 3.2) and towards indirect and long-term effects (see 3.5). Amongst the core ideas in this respect is the view that mass media have their most direct effect by providing the substance of knowledge and judgement on matters which are outside personal experience. We acquire the 'raw material', as it were, with which to form opinions, we receive an indication of what to have opinions about (4.2), and of what the dominant view on these questions is in our own society (4.4). The effects of the mass media will thus depend on the nature of knowledge and belief disseminated, the degree to which it is systematic or diverse, and the degree of our personal dependence on the mass media as a source (4.3).

Thirdly, and related to this, more attention has been paid to the structure of mass media organizations and overall media systems, to collective properties of media professions and of audiences and less to individual communicators and 'receivers' (Ch. 6 in general).

Fourthly, while early communication models dealt with purposeful mass communication and overt content, subsequently there has been more attention paid to latent meaning, unintended bias and the unintended consequences of following production requirements and constraints (6.5 and 6.7).

Fifthly, in line with the early shift away from sender-oriented communication models discussed above, there has been a greater emphasis on the audience as initiator and interpreter of the communication link in mass communication. This development is illustrated in the chapter on the uses and gratifications of mass media (5.1 and 5.2).

Sixthly, compared to earlier times there has been an increasing attention to the sources of mass communication and not only its effects. This is partially reflected in the models of journalistic newsprocessing taken from the work of Gieber and Johnson (6.3) and of Bass (6.6).

1.8 FUTURE DEVELOPMENTS

While the possibility exists of representing the whole process of mass communication, incorporating these developments, in the form of a model of the kind supplied in earlier days by Schramm or Maletzke, it is clear that any such overall model would have to be very complex and would certainly be rather hard to 'read'. At worst, it might be seriously misleading, on two main counts. Firstly, because different approaches to the study of mass communication involve incompatible differences of emphasis and sometimes inconsistencies of theory. Consequently, any single overall model might confuse alternative scientific perspectives and misrepresent the true state of thinking at the present time.

Secondly, a single overall model might implicitly confirm the existence of a single discrete process of communication from society as source to society as audience (terms borrowed from Elliott 1972). In many instances, no such discrete process can be discerned, since we are dealing with several different processes, each open to explanation in its own terms and connected with activities which lie beyond the scope of mass communication. One such set of activities has to do with the arrangements by which society gains access to, and controls, the mass communication system. Secondly, there is a more or less autonomous process by which media organizations obtain, produce and disseminate 'content', according to imperatives which may have little to do with communication in its most usual sense of transmitting meaning to others. Finally, there is a process whereby people choose from and make use of the media in line with interests and needs which are defined according to wider cultural and social experience. It is relatively rare for original source, mass communicator and audience member to be united and co-operating in the same activity with a common perception of it at the same time or in a connected sequence.

For these and other reasons, we do not anticipate an end-point which will produce an ultimate or definitive model embracing all sub-processes in a single view. Rather, we want to stress the utility of model-making as a continuing activity designed to clarify new ideas and theories, to help to organize research findings and point to questions for research. It is also an activity which helps to adapt the scientific study of communication to changes in the reality of communication.

Three topics in particular can be mentioned as deserving attention in the immediate future. Firstly, as we noted at the start, we are already entering a phase where the boundary separating out mass communication from other communication processes is becoming once more less clear. It is not so much the boundary with conversation which is becoming less clear as the boundary with other kinds of information processing and delivery systems, especially those which are telephone and/or computer based. The 'ideal type' of a centralized broadcasting or publishing organization sending out the same content to large and stable 'audiences' is already becoming less appropriate. It is not at all clear how far and in what ways the emerging technological and organizational possibilities will be taken up, but the whole 'map' of communication flow is likely to change with the emergence of new communication functions and expectations. Existing models are clearly inadequate to deal with any of the several possible futures which are not too far away, if only because the clear separation between a collective 'sender' and a collective 'receiver' no longer holds good under conditions of greater flexibility and diversity.

A second topic area in which model-building can play a part as an aid to systematizing evidence and guiding theory, is that of international communication. The elements of a model of relationships and linkages are already present in the terms in which international communication flows are discussed, but the shape of the model depends on an adequate formulation of theory and the accumulation of more data. Thirdly, there is likely to be scope for a further development of models of media institutions which could include economic and power relationships in given national societies. An early attempt in such a direction appears as 6.1, where we compare free enterprise, social market and socialist systems of media control and operation. But much remains to be done to deal with different types of content and to take account of less global but still important differences between national systems. In each of these topic areas, we would expect there to be more than one model, reflecting alternative possibilities of organizing the evidence and alternative political theories and beliefs. In anticipating these future developments, we are again inclined to emphasize our rejection of the idea of a single comprehensive model.

References

Deutsch, K. (1966) *The Nerves of Government*. New York: Free Press.

Elliott, P.H. (1972) *The Making of a Television Series*. London: Constable.

Gerbner, G. (1967) 'Mass media and human communication theory' in Dance, F.E.X. (ed.), *Human Communication Theory*. New York: Holt, Rinehart and Winston.

Janowitz, M. (1968) 'The study of mass communication' in Sills, D.E. (ed.), *International Encyclopedia of the Social Sciences*. New York: Macmillan and Free Press, vol. 3, p. 41.

Osgood, C.E., **Suci, G.J.** and **Tannenbaum, P.H.** (1957) *The Measurement of Meaning*. Urbana: University of Illinois Press.

Theodorson, S.A. and **Theodorson, A.G.** (1969) *A Modern Dictionary of Sociology*. New York: Cassell.

Johnson, F.C. and **Klare, G.R.** (1961) 'General models of communication research: a survey of a decade', *Journal of Communication*, **11**: 13–26.

2 BASIC MODELS

2.1 THE LASSWELL FORMULA

The American political scientist Harold D. Lasswell began an article in 1948 with perhaps the most famous single phrase in communication research: 'A convenient way to describe an act of communication is to answer the following questions:

Who
Says What
In Which Channel
To Whom
With What Effect?'

This has ever since been known and cited as the Lasswell Formula, and if transformed to a graphic model it gives the diagram as in Fig. 2.1.1.

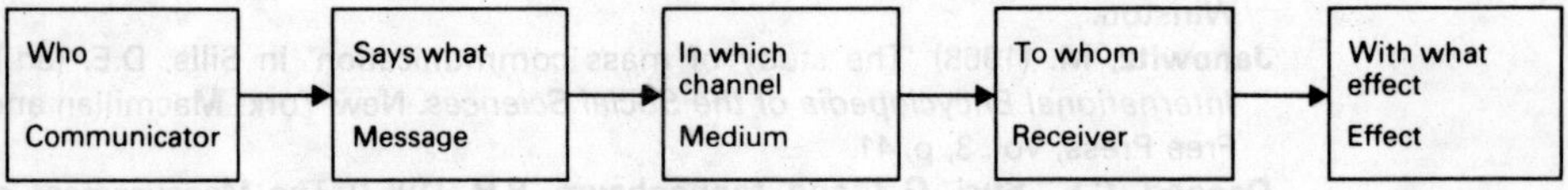

Fig. 2.1.1 The Lasswell Formula with corresponding elements of the communication process (after Lasswell 1948).

This simple formula has been used in several ways, mostly to organize and to give structure to discussions about communication (cf. Riley and Riley 1959). Lasswell himself uses it to point out distinct types of communication research. To each question he has attached a particular type of analysis as is visualized in Fig. 2.1.2.

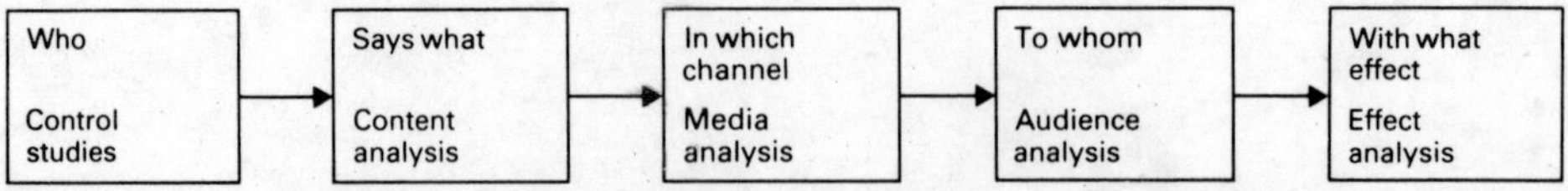

Fig. 2.1.2. The Lasswell Formula with corresponding fields of communication research

Having found the Lasswellian model useful although somewhat too simple, some researchers have developed it further. Braddock (1958) found that there are more considerations to work with than those five presented by Lasswell.

In his version of the model, Braddock adds two more facets of the communicative act, namely the circumstances under which a message is sent, and for what purpose the communicator says something. We may represent this as in Fig. 2.1.3.

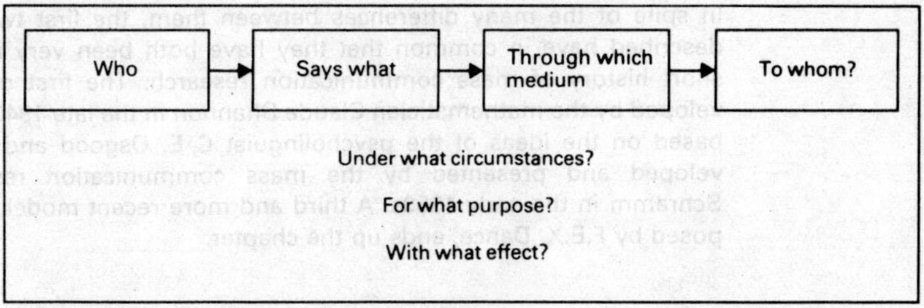

Fig. 2.1.3. Braddocks extension of the Lasswell Formula

Comment The Lasswell Formula shows a typical trait of early communication models: it more or less takes for granted that the communicator has some intent in influencing the receiver and, hence, that communication should be treated mainly as a persuasive process. It is also assumed that messages always have effects. Models such as this have surely contributed to the tendency to exaggerate the effects of, especially, mass communication. On the other hand, this is not surprising when we know that Lasswell's interest at the time was political communication and propaganda. For analysing political propaganda, the formula is well suited.

Braddock stresses that the formula may be misleading in that it directs the researcher to distinct fields of study. In reality they are to a large extent interrelated.

Lasswell has further been criticized for having omitted the element of feedback. In this way, too, his model reflects the general view of the time when it was formulated.

This criticism, however, should not obscure the fact that it is even today a convenient and comprehensive way of introducing people to the study of the communication process.

References

Braddock, R. (1958) 'An extension of the "Lasswell Formula"', *Journal of Communication*, **8**: 88–93.

Lasswell, H.D. (1948) 'The structure and function of communication in society' in Bryson, (ed.), *The Communication of Ideas.* New York: Harper and Brothers.

Riley, J.W. and **Riley, M.W.** (1959) 'Mass communication and the social system' in Merton, R.K., Broom, L. and Cottrell, S. (eds), *Sociology Today*, New York: Basic Books.

2.2 SHANNON AND WEAVER'S, OSGOOD AND SCHRAMM'S, AND DANCE'S MODELS

In spite of the many differences between them, the first two models to be described have in common that they have both been very influential in the short history of mass communication research. The first of them was developed by the mathematician Claude Shannon in the late 1940s. The second is based on the ideas of the psycholinguist C. E. Osgood and was further developed and presented by the mass communication researcher Wilbur Schramm in the early 1950s. A third and more recent model, the helical, proposed by F.E.X. Dance, ends up the chapter.

Shannon and Weaver

Johnson and Klare (1961) say in their review of communication models:

> Of all single contributions to the widespread interest in models today, Shannon's is the most important. For the technical side of communication research, Shannon's mathematical formulations were the stimulus to much of the later effort in this area.

We will not discuss here the mathematical aspects of Shannon's work. Let us just note that he worked for the Bell Telephone Laboratory and that his theories and models primarily applied to its particular field of communication, involving questions such as: Which kind of communication channel can bring through the maximum amount of signals? How much of transmitted signal will be destroyed by noise under way from transmitter to receiver?

These are questions mostly dealt with within the field of information theory. Nevertheless the graphical model, made by Shannon and his co-worker Warren Weaver (1949), has been used analogically by behavioural and linguistic scientists. Technological problems differ of course from human ones, but it is easy to find the traces of the Shannon–Weaver model in a number of later models of human communication.

Communication is here described as a linear, one way process. The model states five functions to be performed and notes one dysfunctional factor, noise. Graphically, it may be presented as in Fig. 2.2.1.

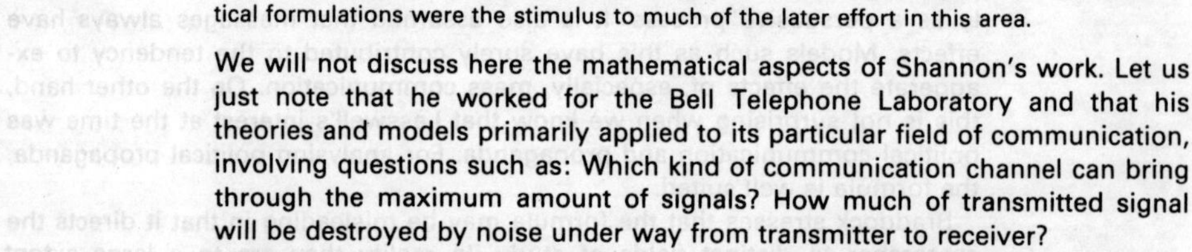

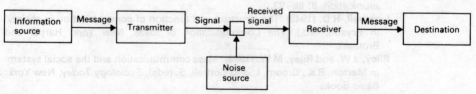

Fig. 2.2.1 Shannon and Weaver's 'mathematical model' describes communication as a linear, one-way process (after Shannon and Weaver 1949).

First in the process is the *information source*, producing a *message* or a *chain of messages* to be communicated.

In the next step, the message is formed into *signals* by a *transmitter*. The signals should be adapted to the *channel* leading to the *receiver*. The function of the receiver is the opposite of that of the transmitter. The receiver reconstructs the message from the signal. The *received message* then reaches the *destination*. The signal is vulnerable in so far as it may be disturbed by *noise*, interference which may occur, for example, when there are many signals in the same channel at the same time. This may result in a difference between transmitted and received signal, which, in its turn, may mean that the message produced by the source and that reconstructed by the receiver and having reached the destination do not have the same meaning. The inability on the part of communicators to realize that a sent and a received message are not always identical, is a common reason why communication fails.

DeFleur's development

DeFleur (1966) developed the Shannon and Weaver model further in a discussion about the correspondence between the meaning of the produced and the received message. He notes that in the communication process, 'meaning' is

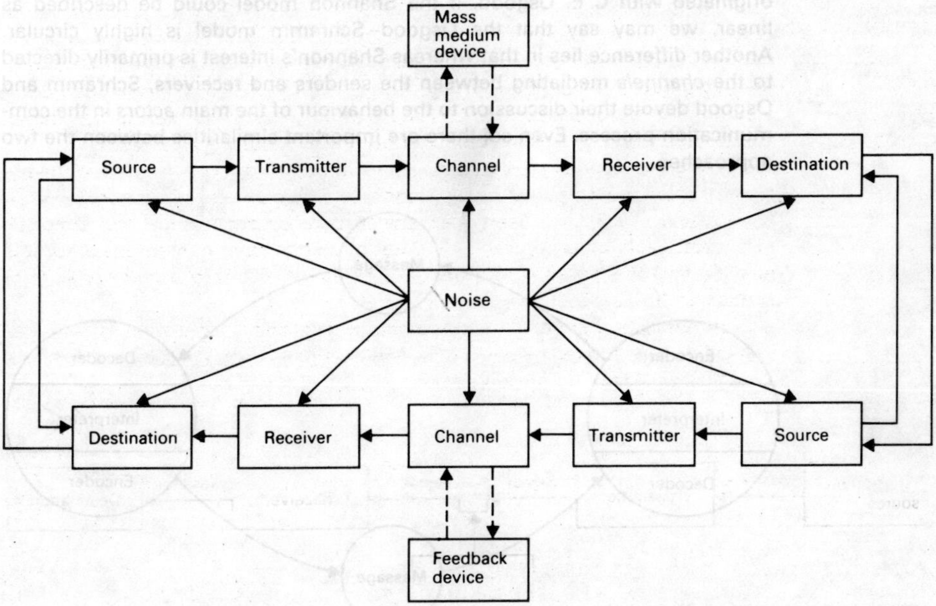

Fig. 2.2.2 DeFleur's development of the Shannon and Weaver model, allowing for feedback (after DeFleur 1970).

transformed into 'message' and describes how the transmitter transforms 'message' into 'information', which then passes through a channel (for example a mass medium). The receiver decodes the 'information' as a 'message', which in its turn is transformed at the destination into 'meaning'. If there is a correspondence between the two 'meanings' the result is communication. But, as DeFleur says, this correspondence is seldom perfect.

In Fig. 2.2.2, DeFleur adds another set of components to the original Shannon and Weaver model to show how the source gets its feedback, which gives the source a possibility of adapting more effectively its way of communicating to the destination. This increases the possibility of achieving correspondence between the meanings (isomorphism).

Shannon and Weaver's model is thus supplemented in an important way. Their model has been criticized for its linearity and lack of feedback. These features are accounted for in DeFleur's version, although it may be noted that in the case of mass communication, the sources (communicators) only get limited or indirect feedback from the audience. We return to this problem again elsewhere in the book (e.g., 2.5, 2.7, 6.3).

The Osgood and Schramm circular model

The next model of this chapter was presented by Wilbur Schramm (1954) and originated with C. E. Osgood. If the Shannon model could be described as linear, we may say that the Osgood–Schramm model is highly circular. Another difference lies in that whereas Shannon's interest is primarily directed to the *channels* mediating between the senders and receivers, Schramm and Osgood devote their discussion to the behaviour of the main *actors* in the communication process. Even so, there are important similarities between the two approaches.

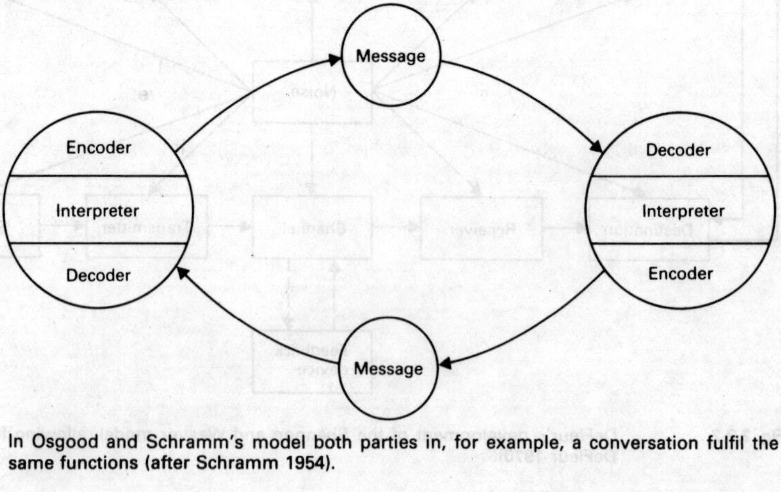

Fig. 2.2.3 In Osgood and Schramm's model both parties in, for example, a conversation fulfil the same functions (after Schramm 1954).

Shannon and Weaver make a distinction between source and transmitter and between receiver and destination. In other words, two functions are fulfilled at the transmitting end of the process and two at the receiving end. In the Schramm–Osgood case, almost the same functions are performed, even if they do not talk about transmitters and receivers (see Fig. 2.2.3). They describe the acting parties as equals, performing identical functions, namely *encoding*, *decoding* and *interpreting*. Roughly, the encoding function is similar to the transmitting, the decoding to the receiving. Schramm and Osgood's interpreting function is fulfilled in Shannon and Weaver's model by the source and the destination. (For a discussion of the terms of the model, see 1.3.)

Comment The traditional linear communication model clearly fixes and separates the roles of sender and receiver and it has from time to time been criticized for doing so. In a comment, Schramm (1954) remarks that

> In fact, it is misleading to think of the communication process as starting somewhere and ending somewhere. It is really endless. We are little switchboard centers handling and rerouting the great endless current of information . . .

The emergence of this approach meant a clear break with the traditional linear/one-way picture of communication. The model is especially useful in describing interpersonal communication but is less suitable for cases without, or with little, feedback. Mass communication is such a case and we can see in section 2.6 how Schramm modifies this model to make it adequate for describing mass communication.

A possible point of criticism of this model would lie in the argument that the model conveys a feeling of equality in communication. Very often communication is, on the contrary, fairly unbalanced as far as communication resources, power and time given to communicate are concerned.

Dance's helical model

Dance's helical model of communication is more recent, compared to the two models earlier presented in this chapter, and it is presented here solely because it may be seen as an interesting development of the Osgood and Schramm circular model.

In a discussion about linear versus circular communication models, Dance (1967) notes that today most people would regard the circular approach as that most adequate for describing the communication process. But it has its shortcomings as well. It

> suggests that communication comes back, full circle, to exactly the same point from which it started. This part of the circular analogy is manifestly erroneous . . .

The helix provides understanding in some cases where the circle fails. It directs one's attention to the fact that the communication process moves forward and that what is communicated now will influence the structure and content of communication coming later on.

Most models in this volume give a sort of 'frozen' picture of the communication process. Dance underlines the *dynamic* nature of communication (see

Fig. 2.2.4). The communication process, like all social processes, contains elements, relations and environments that are continuously changing. The helix describes how different aspects of the process change over time. In a conversation, for example, the cognitive field is constantly widening for the parties or actors involved. The actors get continuously more and more information about the actual topic, about the other's point of view, knowledge etc.

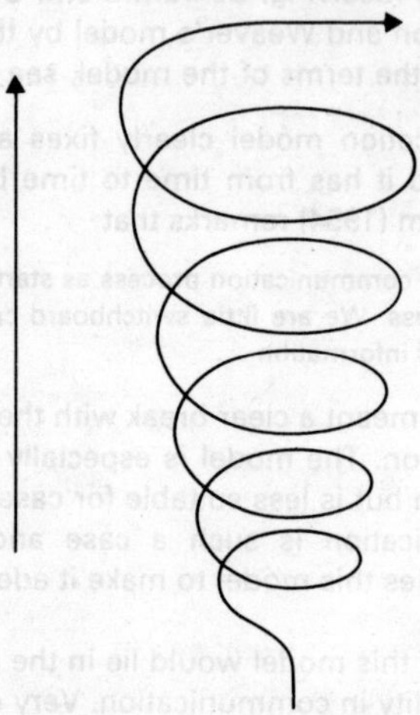

Fig. 2.2.4 Dance's helical model, showing the dynamic nature of the communication process (after Dance 1967).

The helix takes on different shapes in different situations and for different individuals. For some, the helix tends to widen very much, because of prior knowledge of the topic, whereas for others with little basic knowledge, the helix expands moderately. The model may be used to illustrate information gaps (see 4.5 below) and the thesis that knowledge tends to create more knowledge. It may also illustrate communication situations such as the one where a lecturer in a series of lectures on the same subject assumes that his audience becomes successively better informed, which enables him in every new lecture to take this for granted and to structure his presentation accordingly.

Comment Dance's model is, of course, not a tool for detailed analysis. Its worth lies in that it reminds us of the dynamic nature of communication, something that is otherwise too easily forgotten.

It would not go too far to say that the concept of the 'communicating man' here is more positive than in most other models. One gets the notion from this model that man, when communicating, is active, creative and able to store information, whereas many other models depict the individual rather as a passive creature.

References **Dance, F. E. X.** (1967) 'A helical model of communication' in Dance, F. E. X. (ed.), *Human Communication Theory*. New York; Holt, Rinehart and Winston.

DeFleur, M. L. (1966) *Theories of Mass Communication*. New York: David McKay.

Johnson, F. C. and **Klare, G.R.** (1961) 'General models of communication research: a survey of a decade', *Journal of Communication*, **11**: 13–26.

Schramm, W. (1954) 'How communication works' in Schramm, W. (ed), *The Process and Effects of Mass Communication*. Urbana: University of Illinois Press.

Shannon, C. and **Weaver, W.** (1949) *The Mathematical Theory of Communication*. Urbana: University of Illinois Press.

2.3 GERBNER'S GENERAL MODEL OF COMMUNICATION

As the title indicates, the aim of the American mass media researcher George Gerbner has been to sketch a model with a wide range of applications. It was first presented in 1956.

A special feature of this model is that it may be given different shapes depending on what kind of communication situation it describes. Its parts can be used as building blocks, which make it possible to describe simple as well as complicated communication processes as one of production (of messages) and of perception (of messages and of events to communicate about). The model allows us to put forward questions about the nature of and interplay between perception and production.

The model is given a verbal as well as a graphic version, and although we will concentrate on the latter, here is Gerbner's almost Lasswellian (see p. 10) formula:

1. Someone
2. perceives an event
3. and reacts
4. in a situation
5. through some means
6. to make available materials
7. in some form
8. and context
9. conveying content
10. with some consequence

Not all of these stages and elements appear in the basic graphic model (Figs. 2.3.1 and 2.3.2), which, anyhow, may be said to start with an act of perception. What is perceived (Fig. 2.3.1) is marked E (event) and the perceiver, M, perceives the event as E^1. When the model refers to human communication, M may be a man, in a non-human context M may be a machine of some sort (as a thermostat in a heating system).

The relation between E, M and E^1 is one of perception, and as students of mass communications we may use different approaches to this relation. Gerbner discusses a dimension of approaches with two extremes. One extreme is the 'transactional' in which E^1 primarily is regarded as a function of M's 'assumptions, point of view, experiential background and other related factors'. What E^1 will look like to M depends, thus, on factors within or tied to M. The other extreme Gerbner labels 'psychophysical'. There E in itself is the most important factor, giving rise to a perception of 'fidelity and adequacy under favourable conditions'.

What will be perceived by M is determined by his way of selecting, the context in which the E in question is to be found and the degree of availability of this and other E's.

In the next step of the model it is assumed that M wants to communicate about E^1 to someone else. M produces message SE (statement about event).

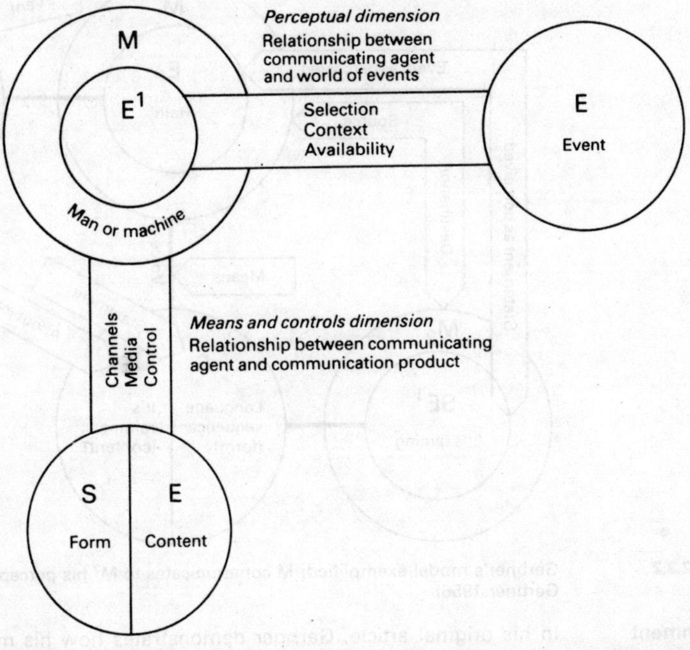

Fig. 2.3.1 Gerbner's general model of communication: M perceives E as E^1 (after Gerbner 1956).

S here stands for 'shape, form', while E is 'content'. Gerbner notes that 'S never stands by itself, unless it signifies noise; it is always coupled with E, the representational, content qualities of the signal . . .'

To send his SE, M is dependent upon channels – media over which he has control to a higher or a lower degree.

The message (SE) may in its turn be perceived by another communication agent (M^2). In the same way as E was perceived by M as E^1, SE will be perceived by M^2 as SE^1. What was said earlier about different ways of approaching perception is valid for the relation $SE–M^2 – SE^1$ as well. We can now see how the model is built up as a perception-production-perception chain, exemplified by Gerbner as in Fig. 2.3.2. The event, condensation of moisture in the air, is perceived by M as 'rain', which gives rise to the statement about the event, 'it's raining', which in turn is perceived or understood by M^2 as 'it's raining'.

This model suggests that the human communication process may be regarded as subjective, selective, variable and unpredictable and that human communication systems are open systems.

The two different approaches to perception discussed above may easily be exemplified in mass communication research, in which given stimuli were expected to produce a predictable quantity of response, whereas one can notice that today's research more readily accepts the 'transactional' way of looking at perception.

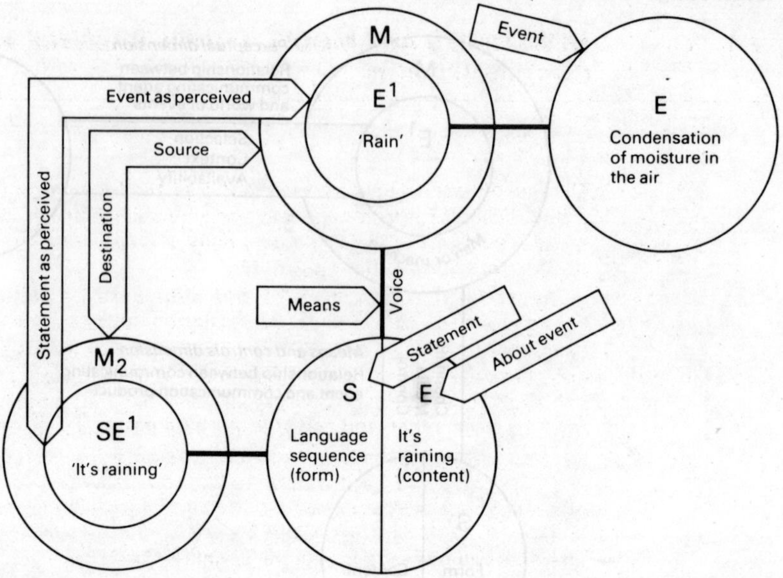

Fig. 2.3.2 Gerbner's model exemplified: M communicates to M^2 his perception of the weather (after Gerbner 1956).

Comment In his original article, Gerbner demonstrates how his model can be used for several purposes. It may, for example, be built to describe mixed human and mechanical communication. It is also used to distinguish between different areas of research and theory building, just as Lasswell used his formula. Gerbner (1964) drew on his own model to illustrate and explain the main procedures of content analysis.

The dynamic character of this model makes it useful on different levels. On the individual-to-individual level it may, for example, be useful to illustrate communicative and perceptual problems in the psychology of witnessing before a court: How adequate is the perception of witness M of event E, and how well is E^1 expressed in SE, and to what degree does the perception SE^1 of judge M^2 correspond to SE?

On a societal level, let E be potential news or just reality, let M stand for mass media, SE for media content and M^2 for media audience. We then have a model that gives us the possibility of asking questions such as 'How good is the correspondence between reality and the stories (between E and SE) about reality given by the media (M)' and 'How well is media content (SE) understood by the media audience (M^2)?' (cf. Gerbner 1964).

References **Gerbner, G.** (1956) 'Toward a general model of communication', *Audio-Visual Communication Review* **4**: 171–99.

Gerbner, G. (1964) 'On content analysis and critical research in mass communication' in Dexter, L.A. and White, D.M. (eds), *People, Society and Mass Communications*. New York: The Free Press.

2.4 NEWCOMB'S ABX MODEL, OTHER 'BALANCE' MODELS AND CO-ORIENTATION

The main model to be discussed in this section is a very simple representation of the dynamics of communicative relationships between two individuals, but it lies at the heart of a wide-ranging body of ideas about attitude change, public opinion formation and propaganda.

The model shown in Fig. 2.4.1 was formulated by Newcomb (1953) and is an extension of earlier work by the psychologist Heider (1946). Heider had been concerned with the degree of consistency or inconsistency which might exist between two persons in relation to a third person or object. His theory held that in the case of two people who have an attitude of like or dislike towards each other and towards an external object, some patterns of relationship will be balanced (as when two persons like each other and also both like the object) and some will be unbalanced (as when two persons like each other, but one likes the object and the other does not, etc). Further, where there is balance, each participant will resist change and where there is imbalance, attempts will be made to restore 'cognitive' balance.

Heider was mainly concerned with cognitive processes *internal* to either of the two participants and Newcomb's development was to apply the theory to communication *between* two or more people. He postulated a 'strain to symmetry' as a result of which the area of agreement would be widened by engaging in communication. He made the assumption that 'communication performs the essential function of enabling two or more individuals to maintain simultaneous orientations to each other and towards objects of an external environment'. Communication is thus a 'learned response to strain' and we are likely to find 'more' communication activity (information giving, seeking and exchange) under conditions of uncertainty and disequilibrium.

The model takes the form of a triangle, the points of which represent, respectively, two individuals A and B and an object X in their common environment. Both individuals are oriented to one another and to X and communication is conceived of as the process which supports the orientation structure, in the

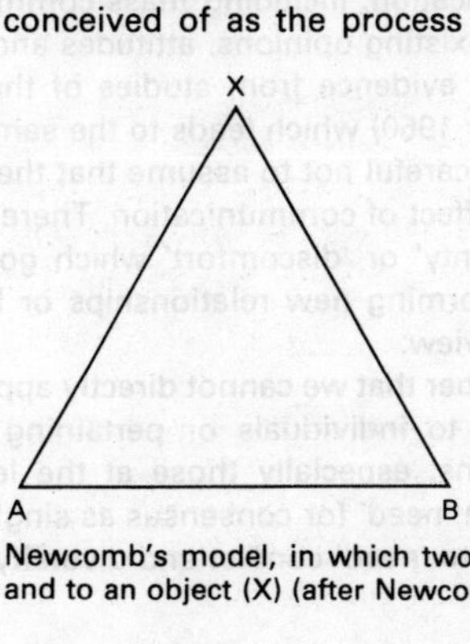

Fig. 2.4.1 Newcomb's model, in which two individuals (A and B) are oriented towards each other and to an object (X) (after Newcomb 1953).

sense of maintaining or improving the symmetry of the relationship between the three elements by transmitting information about any change and by allowing adjustments to occur. The basic assumption of the model is that strain towards consistency of attitude and relationship will instigate communication, where conditions permit.

The main propositions which can be derived from the model are: that discrepancies between A and B in their orientation towards X will stimulate communication: and that the effect of this communication will tend to restore balance, which is postulated as the 'normal state' of a system of relationships.

Subsequently, Newcomb (1959) added some qualifications to his earlier proposition by noting that communication is only likely to be activated under certain conditions: (a) where there is strong attraction between persons; (b) where the object is important to at least one of the participants; and (c) where the object X has a joint relevance for both. Newcomb tested and evaluated this theory by research on the development over time of consensus amongst students who began as strangers and spent time together in the same student accommodation.

Work along similar lines was being carried out at approximately the same time by the social psychologist Festinger (1957), whose theory of cognitive dissonance held that decisions, choices and new information have a potential for creating a feeling of inconsistency for an individual, that such dissonance is 'psychologically uncomfortable' and will motivate the individual concerned to seek information which supports the choice which has been made. An example of the theory in operation is provided by evidence which showed that new car owners read advertisements about the car which they had recently bought more than they read advertisements about other cars.

Comment

In general, the kind of process indicated by the Newcomb model and predicted by balance theory as a whole supports the view that people are likely to attend to sources of information which are in line with their existing positions and look for information which supports and confirms their actual behaviour. It gives weight to theories of selective perception and to the expectation that the most likely effects of communication, including mass communication, will be towards the reinforcement of existing opinions, attitudes and behavioural tendencies. There is independent evidence from studies of the effects of mass communication (e.g. in Klapper 1960) which leads to the same conclusion.

We should, nevertheless, be careful not to assume that the tendency to consensus is the only cause and effect of communication. There is more than one way of resolving the 'uncertainty' or 'discomfort' which goes with cognitive discrepancy, for instance by forming new relationships or by finding further confirmation of divergence of view.

It is also important to remember that we cannot directly apply generalizations relating to processes internal to individuals or pertaining to small groups directly to large-scale situations, especially those at the level of a society. Societies do not have the same 'need' for consensus as single personalities or small groups and may be said to 'need' conflict and diversity in the interest of development.

Co-orientation

More recently, a school of research in communication has flourished which has developed out of the ideas of balance, congruence and seeking of supportive information, which have already been discussed. The label 'co-orientation approach' has been given (by McLeod and Chaffee 1973) to this new tradition, which has its origins both in the work of Newcomb and also in early sociological concerns relating to symbolic interactionism. The key features of the approach are as follows: a focus on interpersonal communication or communication between groups – i.e, on communication which is two-way and interactive; an emphasis on the simultaneous inclusion in any study of the three main elements of information sources, communicators and receivers; an interest in the dynamics of communication situations. The basic features of the approach are illustrated in Fig. 2.4.2 in the form of a kite, which shows the relationship between the elements mentioned in a social setting. (The kite model was first presented on ice at Harlov lake, Sweden, March 1980.)

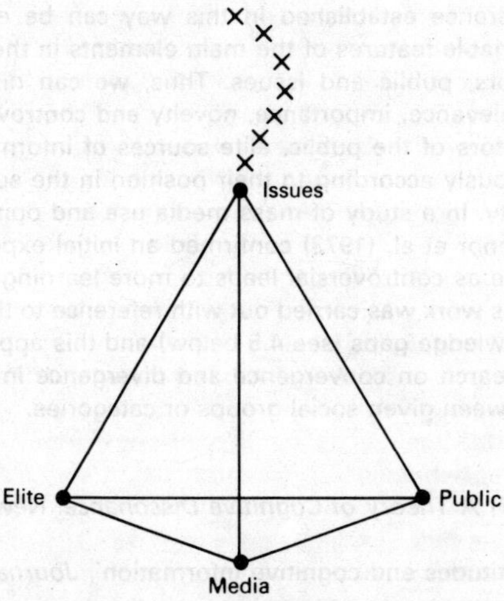

Fig. 2.4.2 A 'kite' co-orientation model, showing the relations between élite, media, public and issue(s).

The elements shown are largely self-explanatory. 'Elite' normally refers to a one-sided political interest. 'Issues' are any matter of current public debate, about which there will be items of information (shown as a set of X's). The public is the relevant community affected and also the audience for the media. In practice 'media' stands for editors, reporters, journalists etc., who deal with public affairs. The lines connecting elements stand for different things: relationships, attitudes and perceptions; one- or two-way channels of communication. There is some correspondence with the Newcomb model (Fig. 2.4.1) in that Elites would be an A, the Public B and the Issues an X. The main differences here are that A and B are now differently motivated role-systems and the element of 'media' has been added as another more or less independent party to the relationship (compare the Westley and MacLean model in the following section).

The model depicts a not uncommon finding of research on public opinion and communication that information about an event or issue is sought from, or acquired by, members of the public, by reference to personal experience, or élite sources, or the mass media, and often from a combination of these. The relevance of theories of interpersonal adjustment and information-seeking just described lies in the fact that the outcome of what is a dynamic situation will depend on the relationships between public and a given élite, on the attitude of the public to the media and on the relationships between élite sources and media channels. Discrepancies between élite and public on issue perception can be a source of strain, leading to attempts to find information from the media and other sources. At the same time, such discrepancies can also lead to attempts by élites to manipulate perceptions by directly acting on events or by trying to control media channels.

The frame of reference established in this way can be enlarged to take account of some variable features of the main elements in the model – élites, media communicators, public and issues. Thus, we can distinguish issues according to their relevance, importance, novelty and controversiality and we can characterize sectors of the public, élite sources of information and mass communicators variously according to their position in the social structure of community or society. In a study of mass media use and opinion about community issues, Tichenor et al. (1973) confirmed an initial expectation that the definition of an issue as controversial leads to more learning from the media about that issue. This work was carried out with reference to the existence and development of knowledge gaps (see 4.5 below) and this approach is particularly relevant to research on convergence and divergence in opinion and information levels between given social groups or categories.

References

Festinger, L.A. (1957) *A Theory of Cognitive Dissonance*. New York: Row and Peterson.

Heider, F. (1946) 'Attitudes and cognitive information', *Journal of Psychology*, **21**: 107–12.

Klapper, J.T. (1960) *The Effects of Mass Communication*. New York: Free Press.

McLeod, J.M. and **Chaffee, S.H.** (1973), 'Interpersonal approaches to communication research', *American Behavioral Scientist*, **16**: 469–99.

Newcomb, T. (1953) 'An approach to the study of communicative acts', *Psychological Review*, **60**: 393–404.

Newcomb, T. (1959) 'The study of consensus' in Merton, R.K., Broom, L. and Cottrell, S. (eds), *Sociology Today*. New York: Basic Books.

Tichenor, P.J., Rodenkirchen, J.M., Olien, C.N. and **Donohue, G.A.** (1973) 'Community issues, conflict and public affairs knowledge' in Clarke, P. (ed.), *New Models for Communication Research*. Beverly Hills: Sage Publications.

2.5 WESTLEY AND MACLEAN'S CONCEPTUAL MODEL FOR COMMUNICATION RESEARCH

This influential model, dating from 1957, was developed with the intention of ordering existing findings of research and providing a systematic treatment which would be especially appropriate for mass communication research. Its origins lie in social psychology and in theories of balance and co-orientation (e.g., Heider, 1946: Festinger, 1957). Its immediate predecessor lies in the basic model of communicative acts (Newcomb, 1953) which was described in the previous section.

Westley and MacLean were concerned to provide a model which represents the much more complex situation of mass communication, while retaining the systematic and interrelated character of the simple case of co-orientation of two persons in relation to external objects.

Westley and MacLean's adaptation of Newcomb's ABX model

There are two stages in the adaptation, based on the authors' perception of the main differences between mass communication and interpersonal communica-

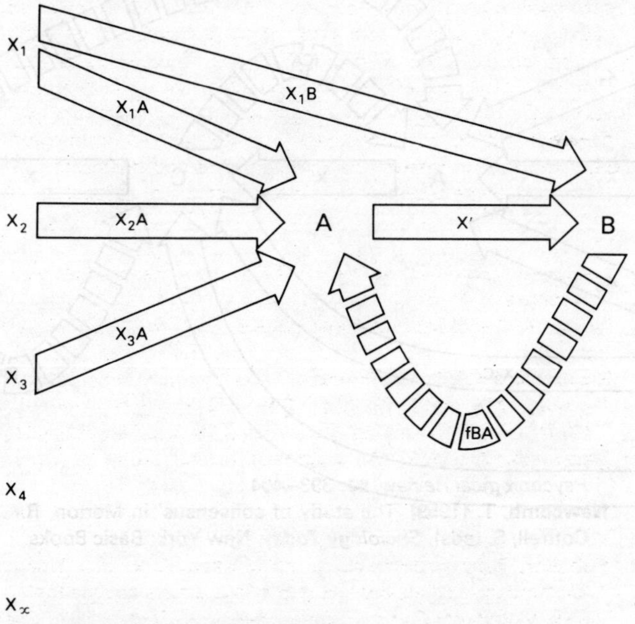

Fig. 2.5.1 First modification of the ABX model, in which A selects from potential X's to communicate with B (after Westley and MacLean 1957).

tion. These differences are:

(a) the fact that in mass communication the possibilities for feedback are minimized or delayed;

(b) the larger number of A's (alternative media sources) and X's (objects in the environment) to which a given individual B (as an audience member) must be oriented and amongst which he has to select.

The basic situation in general communication is represented by a first adaptation of the Newcomb model in the form shown in Fig. 2.5.1.

At this point, the model shows the activity of a source of information, A, selecting from the confusion of X's to communicate with B. In addition, B can have some direct perception of an X (X B) and can respond, by the feedback link (FBA). This would represent a common case in interpersonal communication, where information is being given by one individual to another or sought by an individual from an expert source.

The second modification (Fig. 2.5.2) involves an additional element, the channel role, C, which stands for the mass communicator. This additional role acts as the 'gatekeeper' for the transmission of messages about the environment between A and B. In this version of the model, A stands for a source in society and B for a member of the society. The channel role is conceived of as having an impartial task of interpreting the needs of B and then satisfying them

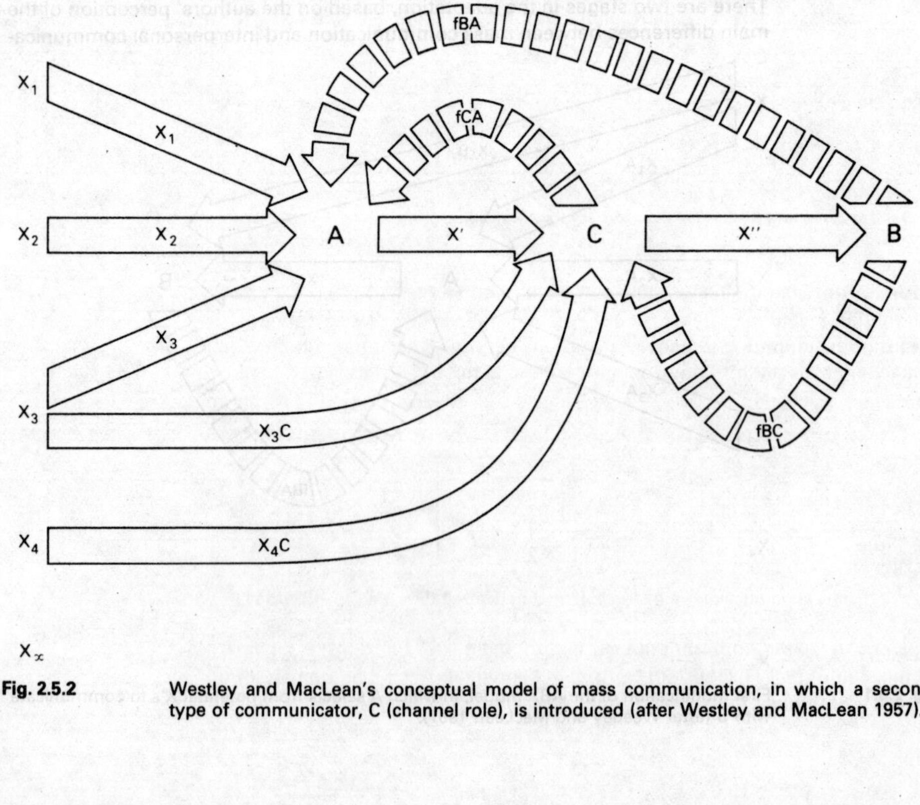

Fig. 2.5.2 Westley and MacLean's conceptual model of mass communication, in which a second type of communicator, C (channel role), is introduced (after Westley and MacLean 1957).

by transforming meaning into a shared symbol system (encoding) and transmitting messages to B by way of a channel or medium.

The main components of the model can now be described as they correspond to the normal mass communication situation.

X stands for any event or object in the social environment, about which communication takes place by way of the mass media (for instance, price changes, political crises, election results and so on).

A is described as an 'advocate' role and refers to the position of individuals or organizations which have something to say about X's to the public as a whole. They might be politicians or advertisers, or news sources. The assumption built into the term 'advocate' is that A's are *purposive* communicators.

C is the media organization or the individual within it, who selects amongst the A's for access to the channel reaching the audience, according to criteria of perceived relevance to audience interests and needs. They may also select directly amongst the X's for communicating to B (the audience). An implied aspect of the C role is that it serves as an agent of the needs of B, as well as for A. Essentially, this role is *non-purposive*, there is no communicative purpose, except as part of a general aim of satisfying the needs of B.

B represents the audience or 'behavioural' role and can stand either for individual or group, or even a social system, to which needs for information or orientation to an environment, can be attributed.

X′ is the choice made by the communicator (C) for access to the channel and X″ is the message as modified in the media organization for transmission to the audiences.

fBA is the feedback from member of the public (B) to the original source (A). This might, for instance, be a vote for a political party or a purchase of a product.

fBC is the feedback from audience member to communication organization, either by way of direct contact, or by means of audience research. Over time this feedback guides future selections and transmissions on the part of C.

fCA is feedback from communicator to advocate. This may either encourage or modify, or reject the attempt at purposive communication by A.

X_{3c} etc. stands for observations amongst X's made directly by mass communication organization, for instance an eyewitness account by a reporter.

The model is important for drawing attention to a number of significant and distinctive aspects of the mass communication process:

The several stages at which selection takes place: amongst aspects of the environment by 'advocates' who might be experts or genuine opinion leaders; amongst the advocates by the mass communicators; amongst the events or objects of the real world by mass communicators; amongst the message transmitted by communicators, on the part of members of the audience.

The self-regulating character of the system, arising from the (presumed) diversity of C roles. This should guarantee that the needs of B for relevant messages are met, since competition between C's for attention should ensure that reality is adequately conveyed.

The distinction between purposive and non-purposive communication, both of which occur in mass communication. The former is here represented primarily by the advocate role. Where A communicates non-purposively about an X, then A simply becomes another X. In this model, the actions of C are generally thought to be non-purposive, except insofar as these actions mediate or serve the needs of advocates or audience. Earlier models seem not to allow for the very common circumstance of 'directionless' communication. In this model, the allocation of purpose can be made at either end, as the motives of the audience or those of the would-be communicators.

The importance of feedback (or its absence), usually from the audience (B) to either A or C. In the terms of this model, it is feedback which helps to ensure the systematic character of the relationship between participants.

The model is intended to illustrate a situation where links between X or A on the one hand and B on the other are not monopolized by one C role. B may have other direct links with A (e.g. through membership of an organization) and may have direct experience of X (e.g. price rise, change in weather).

Applications of the model

The main use of the model is to help in posing questions for research about real mass communication situations, and especially about the mass communicator or media organization. For instance, it suggests the following questions. What are the relevant characteristics of those who occupy C roles (the mass communicators)? How independent are C's from each other? What criteria are applied by C in allocating access to either X's or A's? How adequately are the needs of B interpreted? In what ways are messages about X's altered in passing through the C position in the communication chain? These questions are all fundamental to much research on communicators and their organizations and such research has grown in volume since the model was first published. The model has been cited in several studies of gatekeeping and used in a number of empirical and conceptual studies (e.g. Gieber 1960; Blumler 1970; McNelly 1959).

A good example of the application of the model can be found in Blumler's (1970) analysis of the relationship between politicians, television broadcasters and the electorate in Britain. The advocate (A) role equates with that of the politician who wants to use television (C role) to reach the voters (B role). The situation contains elements of tension because access has to be limited and because there is a potential conflict between broadcasters' wish to please and serve the public and the claims of different political interests over television as a channel to voters. The tension has been increased by the growing importance of television as a means of political communication and the increasing public expectation that television should be not only a channel for political messages, but also a source of criticism, scrutiny or guidance in the public interest. Thus conflict is located mainly in relations between A and C. It is further accentuated in the case of public broadcasting systems by the clash between broadcasters' wish for independence and their formal accountability to the public by way of the political system. The model proved very useful in directing attention to the main points at issue in this case and it could equally provide a useful framework for comparisons over time or between different political systems.

Comment

Despite its theoretical and practical value, there are some problems with the model which should be noted. Firstly, in its original presentation, it involved the assumption that such a system of relationships, like that in the original Newcomb model, would be self-regulating and mutually beneficial to all participants. It would balance the interests of senders and receivers, given free operation. In practice, the relationship of the three main participants is rarely balanced and is not only a communication relationship. There is also a political relationship between A and C, and therefore sometimes one between C and B. Thus, as we saw in the example, A may have some power over C and nearly always C depends to some extent on the A role to supply information without which it cannot operate.

A second main weakness is that the model overemphasizes the degree of integration of the mass communication process and the degree to which 'advocates', communicators and audience share the same view of the process. In practice, each may be pursuing objectives which have often little to do with each other. 'Advocates' may send messages without really wishing or needing to communicate, communicators can follow organizational aims of their own and audience members may be mainly spectators of whatever is shown to them, without having 'needs' of a specific kind which communicators have to meet. The model is thus idealist and somewhat normative in offering what is essentially a free market version of the communicator role.

Thirdly, the model overstates the independence of the communicator from the society, especially in political matters or those which concern the interests of the state. For example, Tracey (1977) suggests that there are different possible forms of interrelationship between the three elements of state/commercial structure; broadcasting institution; and public. In one version, the first two elements are assimilated and reflect a tendency by the state or economic power sources to 'colonize' the broadcasting institution or the 'fourth estate' in general.

References

Blumler, J.G. (1970) 'Television and politics' in Halloran, J.D. (ed.), *The Effects of Television*. London: Panther Books.

Festinger, L. A. (1957) *A Theory of Cognitive Dissonance*. New York: Row and Peterson.

Gieber, W. (1960) 'Two communicators of the news: a study of the roles of sources and reporters', *Social Forces*, **37**: 76–83.

Heider, F. (1946) 'Attitudes and cognitive information', *Journal of Psychology*,

21: 107–12.
McNelly, J. (1959) 'Intermediary communicators in the flow of news', *Journalism Quarterly*, **36**: 23–6.
Newcomb, T. (1953) 'An approach to the study of communicative acts', *Psychological Review*, 60: 393–404.
Tracey, M. (1977) *The Production of Political Television*. London: Routledge and Kegan Paul.
Westley, B.H. and **MacLean, M.** (1957) 'A conceptual model for mass communication research', *Journalism Quarterly*, **34**: 31–8.

2.6 THE SCHRAMM MODEL OF MASS COMMUNICATION

Even if one accepts the view that the communication process is a circular one – as advocated by, for example, Schramm and Osgood (section 2.2) – one may maintain that some types of communication are more circular and that some are less so than others. Mass communication in general belongs to the latter category. The weak link in the mass communication chain is feedback and in the mass communication version of the Schramm–Osgood model feedback to the media organization is only of an inferential type: 'receivers stop buying the publication, or no longer listen to the program, or cease to buy the product advertised'.

The heart of Schramm's model (Fig. 2.6.1) is the media organization, in which the same functions are fulfilled as in the Schramm–Osgood version, encoding, interpreting and decoding. A newspaper may illustrate this: the paper receives a vast amount of news items and information every day. The newsmen read, evaluate and decide what to pass on to the reader. During this procedure the texts will be modified, rewritten or rejected by those working in the media organization. If the material gets past the gatekeepers it will be printed and distributed.

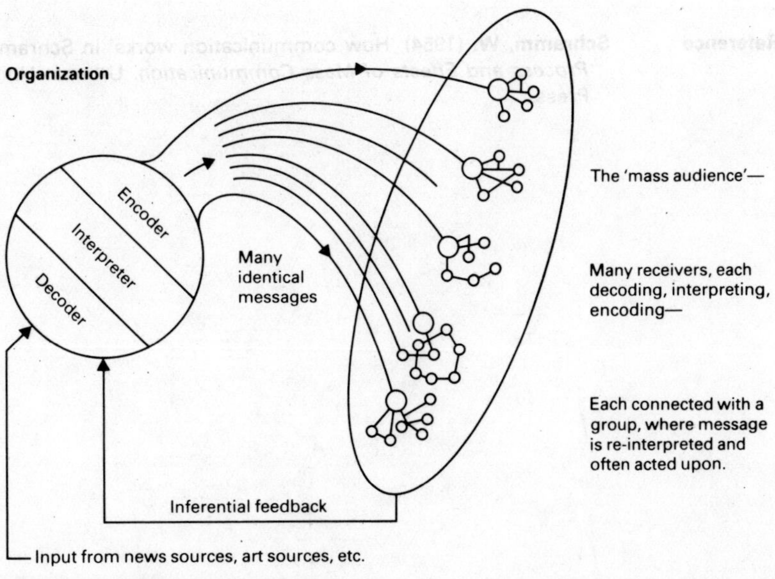

Fig. 2.6.1 Schramm's mass communication model, showing production and reception of mass communications as well as inferential feedback to the medium (after Schramm 1954).

The mass audience, reached by the messages of the media organization, consists of individuals. However, most individuals belong to primary and secondary groups and Schramm (1954) points out that media messages may find their way from the individual receiver to members of surrounding groups. This process is further described in section 3.3 below (interpersonal influence), where it is suggested, amongst other things, that mass media content has its greatest effects when filtered by way of individuals and groups.

One may add in reference to the Schramm mass communication model that the decoding-interpreting-encoding work within the media organization is really more complicated than in the model. In reality, the principal decoding-interpreting-encoding processes consist of a great many sub-processes, in which the same functions are performed over and over again.

Comment Seen as a part of the developmental history of communication models, Schramm's mass communication model exemplifies the tendency of going from general communication models to models of *mass* communication and the tendency to look at mass communication as an integrated part of society. Schramm's image of mass media audience members as interacting with other people and groups, discussing and reacting upon mass media messages, may be seen as a reaction against the picture of a mass society where individuals are very loosely connected and where mass communication messages reach, influence and manipulate the members of the audience one by one.

Reference

Schramm, W. (1954) 'How communication works' in Schramm, W. (ed.), *The Process and Effects of Mass Communication*. Urbana: University of Illinois Press.

2.7 TOWARDS A SOCIOLOGICAL VIEW OF MASS COMMUNICATION: RILEY AND RILEY

Early communication models easily give the impression that the communication process takes place in a social vacuum and that influence from the environment is not worth bothering about. Gradually, however, one has come to realize that homo communicus is part of social structures of different kinds. The article 'Mass communications and the social system' by John W. Riley and Mathilda White Riley (1959) is an important step in this progress towards a more sociological view. The article criticizes the traditional view of mass communication which the Rileys considered had failed to explain satisfactorily many of the results of communications research. As a constructive continuation of this criticism they presented what they called a working model. Their aim was to make it possible to analyze mass communication in a more sociological way by regarding mass communication as one social system among others in society.

Riley and Riley describe the traditional view in the following way: the communicator seems always to have the intention of influencing his receivers through transmitting specially designed messages, which should thus be regarded chiefly as stimuli. The receiver is isolated in an unorganized 'mass' and he decides – often on rational grounds – how to react to the message received. Traditionally, researchers do not pay any attention to the importance of those psychological processes which do not come directly within the communication process but which may nevertheless influence its course.

The authors point to the role played in the communication process by primary groups and reference groups. Primary groups are distinguished by intimate relations among their members, a family being a typical example. A reference group is a group with the help of which an individual may define his attitudes, values and behaviour. He does not need to be a member of the group, but its norms will nevertheless guide him. Primary groups close to the individual often serve as reference groups for him as well.

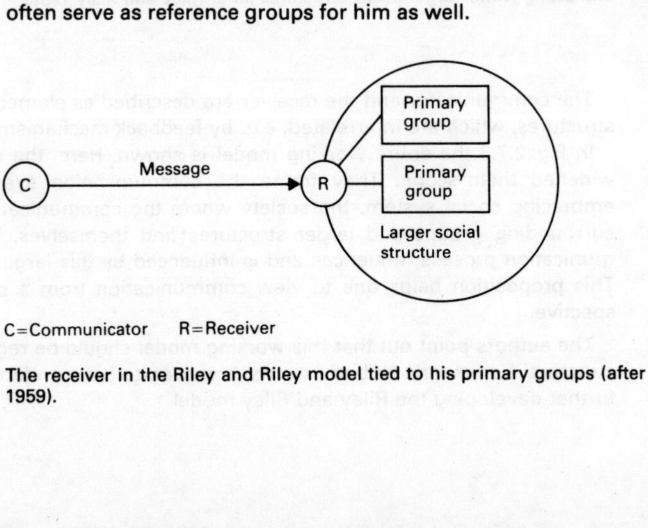

Fig. 2.7.1 The receiver in the Riley and Riley model tied to his primary groups (after Riley and Riley 1959).

As a communicator or a receiver in the communication process, an individual is influenced by the primary group. As a communicator he may be influenced to select and shape his messages in a special way, as a receiver he may be guided by these groups in how to select, perceive and react to messages. In Fig. 2.7.1 we find the communicator and the receiver connected with primary groups.

The primary groups do not, in their turn, function in a social vacuum. The authors regard them instead as parts of a larger social structure. Let us take an example: a student in a school is generally tied to at least one peer group (primary group) which in its turn is part of the class and the school as a whole (the larger social structure). The primary groups are influenced in their attitudes and behaviour partly by each other, partly by this larger structure, which may also influence the individual directly. Within it one finds so-called secondary groups such as political organizations, unions, which serve as norm-givers and guides in the same way as the primary groups.

We get Fig. 2.7.2.

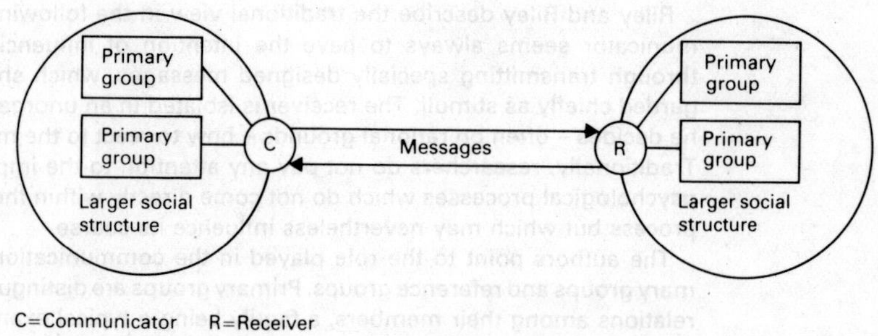

Fig. 2.7.2 Receiver and communicator in the Riley and Riley model connected with primary groups and acting within larger social structures (after Riley and Riley 1959).

The communicator and the receiver are described as elements of two larger structures, which are interrelated, e.g. by feedback mechanisms.

In Fig. 2.7.3 the entire working model is shown. Here, the originators have widened their scope. They frame the communication systems in an all-embracing social system, the society where the communication actors, their surrounding groups and larger structures find themselves. The mass communication process influences and is influenced by this larger social process. This proposition helps one to view communication from a sociological perspective.

The authors point out that this working model should be regarded only as a structural framework. Nobody seems, however, to have undertaken the task of further developing the Riley and Riley model.

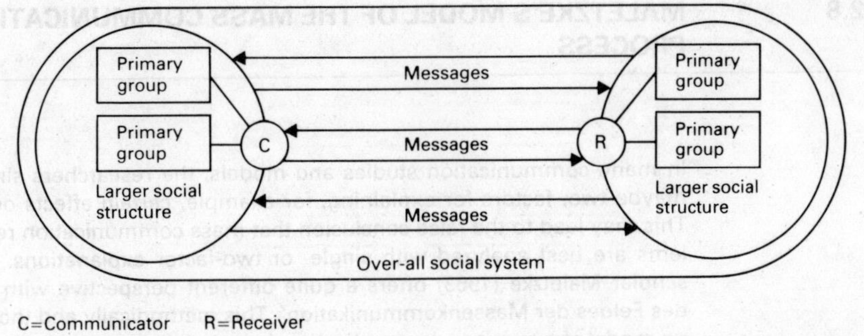

Fig. 2.7.3 Riley and Riley: the communication system framed by a societal system (after Riley and Riley 1959).

Comment The model has surely helped to tie the concept of mass communication to existing sociological theories and has enabled sociological analysis of previously not fully explained research results. Its suggestion that mass communication should be seen as a social process among others and that it may influence and be influenced by the surrounding society is equally important.

The contribution made by the model to new ways of looking at communication effects is important, too. Mendelsohn (1963) mentions the Rileys as two of the originators of 'the new look in mass communication' in that they 'focus on the mediating role of other psychological factors in influencing the impacts that the mass media can produce on individuals and groups'.

References

Mendelsohn, H. (1963) 'Sociological perspectives on the study of mass communication' in Dexter, L.A. and White, D.M. (eds), *People, Society and Mass Communication.* New York: Free Press.

Riley, J.W. and **Riley, M.W.** (1959) 'Mass communication and the social system' in Merton, R.K. et al. (eds), *Sociology Today.* New York: Basic Books.

2.8 MALETZKE'S MODEL OF THE MASS COMMUNICATION PROCESS

In many communication studies and models, the researchers single out one, maybe two, factors for explaining, for example, certain effects or behaviours. This may lead to the false conclusion that mass communication research problems are best analyzed with single- or two-factor explanations. The German scholar Maletzke (1963) offers a quite different perspective with his 'Schema des Feldes der Massenkommunikation'. This methodically and thoroughly built up model shows mass communication as a social psychologically very complicated process, in which explanations are more likely to be of a multi- than of a single-factor type.

As the model is relatively complex and fairly hard to survey, we will first discuss separately the elements, which are later brought together in the complete model.

Maletzke builds his model upon the traditional basic elements, communicator, message, medium and receiver. However, between medium and receiver he has noticed two more components. A 'pressure' or 'constraint' from the medium and the receiver's image of the medium.

In the first case we are being acquainted with the fact that different media demand different kinds of adaptation on the part of the receiver. Every medium has its possibilities and limitations, and the characteristics of the medium must be considered as influencing the way the receiver experiences and is affected by the media content. Thus, we do not experience a play in exactly the same way when it is performed on the radio as when it is performed on TV. McLuhan's (1964) often cited expression 'the medium is the message' may well illustrate how seriously the role of the medium in relation to the receiver is sometimes taken. In this context, Maletzke regards the following medium characteristics as relevant:

(a) The type of perception demanded from the receiver (viewer, reader, etc.);
(b) The extent to which the receiver is bound to the medium spatially and in time;
(c) The social contexts in which members of the audience receive the media content;
(d) The difference in time between event and consumption of the message about the event, i.e. the degree of simultaneity.

The medium image held by the receiver causes expectations of the media content and may thus be assumed to have an influence on the receiver's choice of content as well as on his way of experiencing it and responding to it. The prestige and credibility of the medium are important elements in this image.

The two variables of choice and experience/effect may be seen as important dependent variables or consequences in the process of receiving. Apart from the already mentioned variables of 'medium pressure' or 'medium constraint' and the receiver's image of the medium, some other factors or variables in the model may be labelled as causative or independent in this part of the process.

The receiver's self-image – the individual's perception of himself, his roles, attitudes and values create a disposition in receiving communication. Social psychological research has shown, for example, that we tend to reject information that is inconsistent with values we ascribe to ourselves.

The personality structure of the receiver – social psychologists often assume that some categories of persons are more easily influenced than others. It is thus often said that individuals with a low self-esteem are more easily persuaded than others (see, for example, Hovland and Janis 1959). This should hold true, too, in the mass communication process.

The receiver's social context – this factor may refer to the surrounding society, the community where the receiver lives, the groups he belongs to as well as the individuals with whom he interacts. The significance of the group has been testified to by several students of the communication process. The more the individual accepts being a member of a group, the smaller are the possibilities of influencing his attitudes with messages which run contrary to the values of the group.

Maletzke also notes that the creators of opinion, through whom mass media content is usually passed on, are frequently to be found in the receiver's immediate social surroundings, for instance in his local community.

The receiver as a member of the public: the receiving situation is not the same in mass communication as in face-to-face communication. As a member of the unorganized mass public, the individual receiver does not face any great demands to respond or to act in a certain way as he does in the less anonymous face-to-face situation. The very situation of receiving may influence the

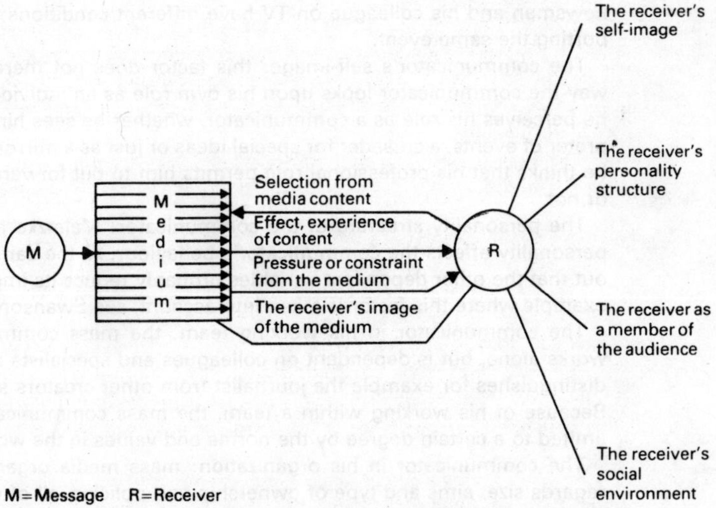

Fig. 2.8.1 The receiver part of the Maletzke model, showing audience behaviour as a result of a number of factors (after Maletzke 1963).

experience. We know, thus, that children experience dramatic mass media content differently if it is consumed together with peers or together with, for example, their parents (Himmelweit et al. 1958).

So far the Maletzke model may be represented graphically as in Fig. 2.8.1. We have hitherto studied the receiver part of the model. Now let us look at the communicator part of it.

In the same way that we regarded the choice and experience of the receiver as dependent variables, there are two such variables related to the communicator. These are the *communicator's choice to transmit what he transmits* and *his way of giving shape to the message*. These two may be labelled the communicator's communicating bahaviour.

The communicator in the mass communication process has, as a rule, more material or potential messages to start with than he will pass on. In such cases he has to sample from the total amount of material according to certain criteria.

When deciding how to structure and give shape to his messages, the communicator is also faced with situations of choice. How the selection and shaping are performed depends among other things on the following factors in the model.

'Pressure' or constraint from the message: the communicator is bound to adapt the shaping of the message to the type of content. A report from a funeral is made differently from a gossip column. A single message may also be regarded as an element of a whole. A news item may be structured in a special way to fit into the whole news programme.

'Pressure' or constraint from the medium: every medium offers the communicator a special combination of constraints and possibilities. The press newsman and his colleague on TV have different conditions to observe in reporting the same event.

The communicator's self-image: this factor does not merely comprise the way the communicator looks upon his own role as an individual but also how he perceives his role as a communicator, whether he sees himself as an interpreter of events, a crusader for special ideas or just as a mirror of events, and if he thinks that his professional role permits him to put forward his own values or not.

The personality structure of the communicator: Maletzke assumes that the personality affects the communicator's behaviour. At the same time he points out that the other dependent variables probably reduce its importance. (For an example where this factor is taken into account, see Swanson 1956.)

The communicator in his working team: the mass communicator seldom works alone, but is dependent on colleagues and specialists around him. This distinguishes for example the journalist from other creators such as novelists. Because of his working within a team, the mass communicator's freedom is limited to a certain degree by the norms and values in the working group.

The communicator in his organization: mass media organizations vary as regards size, aims and type of ownership and policies, all of which are important contextual factors for the individual communicator. As for the policies, some students of mass media organizations have noted that the individual journalist may hold beliefs and attitudes contrary to those of the organization, which may force the newsmen to follow the explicit or implicit rules. However, the communicator/journalist may also have possibilities of getting round them (see for example Breed 1955).

Pressure and constraints caused by the public character of the media content: the fact that the mass media communicator's production is open to inspection by the public puts some constraints, both psychological and legal, on the communicator's work. Often a certain amount of control is exercized by professional associations.

The communicator's social environment: in almost the same way as the social environment of the receiver affects his way of selecting and experiencing the media content, the communicator's way of gatekeeping and shaping the content is dependent on his social surroundings, not only those which the working team and the rest of the organization constitute.

The communicator part of Maletzke's model will look like this graphically (Fig. 2.8.2)

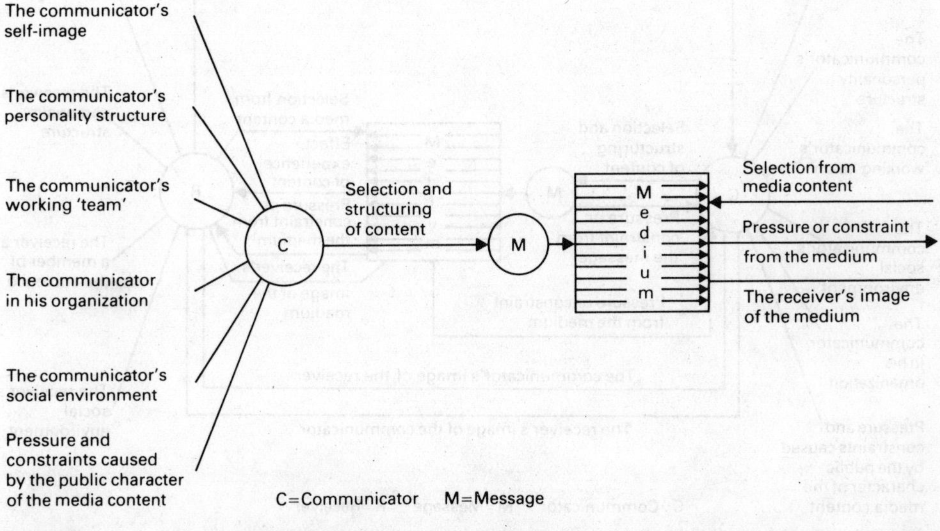

Fig. 2.8.2 The part of the Maletzke model which shows factors influencing communicator behaviour (after Maletzke 1963).

The complete model adds some further relevant factors:

The receiver's and the communicator's image of each other: it is often stressed in communications research, that when creating his messages, the communicator has a picture of the receiver in mind, even if the latter is not physically present (Fearing 1953). For the mass communicator, a certain problem arises because the audience is often heterogenous and anonymous, and because the actual existing feedback provides a weak basis for a true and satisfying image of the audience. This circumstance diminishes the effectiveness of the communication.

We have already noted that the receiver's image of the medium is important for his selection and experience. It is often difficult for the receiver to form a picture of the communicator, but, as is the case in his relation to the medium, the receiver is assumed to be affected by such a factor as the degree of credibility. It is also of importance whether the receiver identifies with the communicator and his values or not.

Spontaneous feedback from the receiver: the mass communication process is mainly to be regarded as a one-way process, in that it mostly lacks the kind of spontaneous feedback that we find in face-to-face communication. As noted above, this lack is one reason for the communicator's (often) inadequate image of the audience.

As all the elements and factors indicated in the Maletzke model have now been treated, we will show the complete model (Fig. 2.8.3).

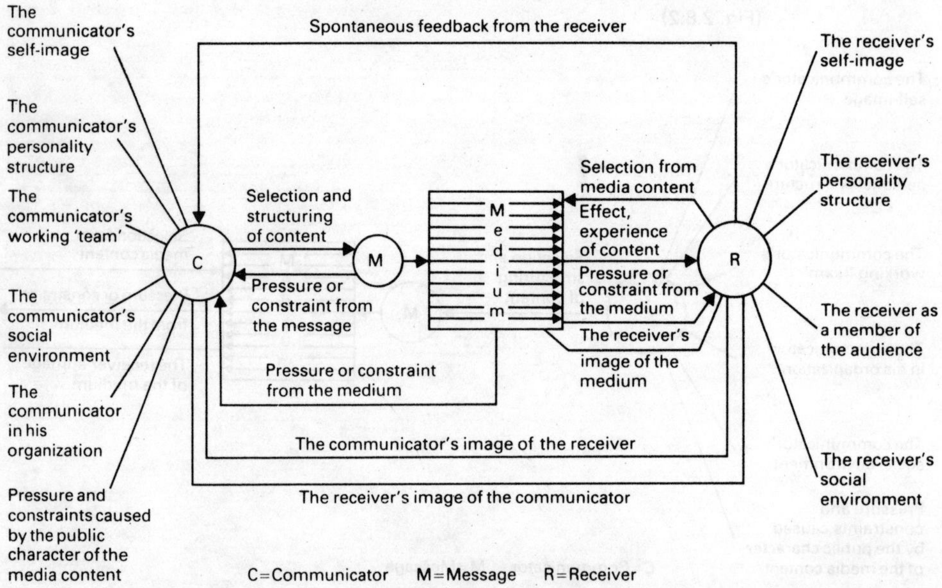

Fig. 2.8.3 The complete Maletzke model (after Maletzke 1963).

Maletzke's image of the mass communicating man – communicator or receiver – is a rather complex one. The behaviour of both communicator and receiver is a function of a large number of factors. This complexity is, no doubt, an important reason why mass communication research has been fairly unsuccessful in explaining and predicting outcomes of the mass communication process.

Comment The model serves as a summing-up of a couple of decades' social psychological interest in mass communication. In spite of its being relatively dated, it is still useful in that it contains a number of important factors and relationships, some of which have not yet been very thoroughly studied.

Being so detailed, the model may well serve as a check list of the relevant factors of the mass communication process, perceived from a social psychological point of view. It may, thus, be used in cases where one wishes to analyse descriptions of such processes.

The Maletzke model has been used by the originator himself when structuring his comprehensive work *Psychologie der Massenkommunikation* (1963), in which every relation, factor and element is thoroughly discussed.

References

Breed, W. (1955) 'Social control in the newsroom: a functional analysis', *Social Forces*, **33**: 326–35.

Fearing, F. (1953) 'Toward a psychological theory of human communication', *Journal of Personality*, **22**: 71–88.

Himmelweit, H. et al. (1958) *Television and the Child*. London: Oxford University Press.

Hovland, C.I. and **Janis, I.L.** (eds) (1959) *Personality and Persuasibility*. New Haven: Yale University Press.

Maletzke, G. (1963) *Psychologie der Massenkommunikation*. Hamburg: Verlag Hans Bredow-Institut.

McLuhan, M. (1964) *Understanding Media*. New York: McGraw-Hill.

Swanson, G. (1956) 'Agitation through the press: a study of the personalities of publicists', *Public Opinion Quarterly*, **20**: 441–56.

3 PERSONAL INFLUENCE, DIFFUSION, AND EFFECTS OF MASS COMMUNICATION ON INDIVIDUALS

3.1 STIMULUS-RESPONSE MODELS AND THEIR MODIFICATIONS

Very much, perhaps even most, of mass communication theorizing has dealt with the question of effects. Effects have been of interest for many groups in society, those who want to reach others with their message and therefore want to get the most effective channel to the audience, and those who express fears for the negative impact of media.

The so-called stimulus-response principle has in this context been one of great importance. According to this simple model of learning, effects are specific reactions to specific stimuli, so that one can expect and predict a close correspondence between media message and audience reaction. The main elements in this model are: (a) a message (stimulus, S); (b) a receiver (organism, O); and (c) the effect (response, R). Usually, the relations between these elements are demonstrated this way:

$$S \rightarrow O \rightarrow R$$

The image of a hypodermic needle was used to represent an early but highly influential mass media version of the effect process. Media content was then seen as injected in the veins of the audience, that was then supposed to react in foreseeable ways.

Behind this conception one would find two main ideas:

1. An image of a modern society as consisting of an aggregate of relatively 'atomized' individuals acting according to their personal interests and little constrained by social ties and constraints;
2. A dominant view of the mass media as engaged in campaigns to mobilize behaviour according to intentions of powerful institutions, whether public or private (advertisers, government bureaucracies, political parties, etc.).

The main features of this 'mass society' stimulus-response model are:

(a) The assumption that messages are prepared and distributed in systematic ways and on a large scale. At the same time, they are 'made available' for attention by many individuals, not directed to particular persons.
(b) The technology of reproduction and neutral distribution is expected to maximize aggregate reception and response.
(c) Little or no account is taken of an intervening social or group structure and a direct contact is made between media campaigner and individual.
(d) All individual recipients of the message are 'equal' in weighting or value – only aggregate numbers count (as voters, consumers, supporters, etc.).

(e) There is an assumption that contact from the media message will be related at some given level of probability to an effect. Thus, contact with the media tends to be equated with some degree of influence from the media, and those not reached are assumed to be unaffected.

DeFleur (1970) has discussed some of the modifications made to the stimulus-response model. One has been called the individual differences theory of mass communication. It implies that media messages contain particular stimulus attributes that have differential interaction with personality characteristics of members of the audience. The revised stimulus-response theory allows for intervening personality variables. Research on propaganda designed to reduce prejudice provides a good illustration of the individual differences theory (Cooper and Jahoda 1947). In this research it turned out that prejudiced people systematically misinterpreted the message of an anti-prejudice cartoon series.

Based primarily on the individual differences theory is the 'psychodynamic model' (DeFleur 1970; Fig. 3.1.1), which rests on the belief that the key to effective persuasion lies in modifying the internal psychological structure of the individual. Through this modification the desired behaviour responses will be achieved.

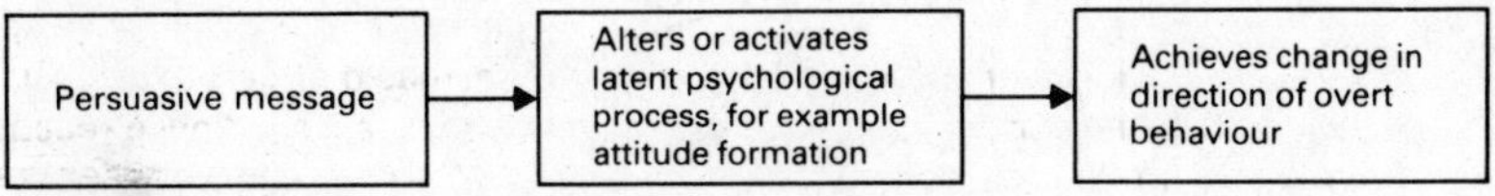

Fig. 3.1.1 DeFleur's psychodynamic model, showing the internal psychological structure as an intervening variable in the effect process (after DeFleur 1970).

The research supporting the model includes a wide range of studies of the existence of more or less 'persuasible' types of personality (e.g. Janis and Hovland 1959) and other work on the dispositions of the receiver and attitudes to the source. DeFleur concludes that while the psychodynamic model has not been fully verified, it does seem to work some of the time. Essential to this model is a focus on variables relating to the individual recipient, a retention of the simple cause and effect hypothesis and often a reliance on attitude change as an index of behaviour change.

Comment

Halloran (1969) notes that the 'mechanistic stimulus-response model' is important because 'even in its crudest form it has not entirely disappeared' and 'because it has provided a base from which so much of our thinking about mass communication has stemmed'. This seems to hold true even today, and many researchers blame the stimulus-response principle for having given rise to the notion of the mass communication process merely as a process of persuasion.

Another very common accusation relates the exaggerated ideas about the omnipotence of the mass media to the stimulus-response model.

In spite of the criticism levelled at this model, nobody can deny that it directs our interest to an important part of the mass communication process. Knowing today that the early naive versions of stimulus-response theory give a too simple picture of mass communication, we still cannot reject their modified versions as useless and uninformative.

References

Cooper, E. and **Jahoda, M.** (1947) 'The evasion of propaganda', *Journal of Psychology*, **23**: 15–25.

DeFleur, M. (1970) *Theories of Mass Communication*. New York: David McKay.

Halloran, J.D. (1969) 'The communicator in mass communication research' in Halmos, P. (ed.), *The Sociology of Mass Media Communicators. The Sociological Review* Monograph 13.

Janis, I.L. and **Hovland, C.I.** (1959) *Personality and Persuasibility*. New Haven: Yale University Press.

3.2 COMSTOCK'S PSYCHOLOGICAL MODEL OF TELEVISION EFFECTS ON INDIVIDUAL BEHAVIOUR

This model (Comstock et al. 1978), in its complete form, is an attempt to find an organizing framework for research out of a large and varied set of empirical enquiries into the direct behavioural effects of television, with particular reference to the unintended effects of entertainment content. The emphasis is on effects which might involve aggresive or delinquent behaviour (since that has been the concern of much of such research), but the model could equally accommodate sexual behaviour, general 'prosocial' behaviour and even learning from reality material.

The purpose of the model is to account for, and help predict, the occurrence of an effect on individual behaviour in a given case by bringing together some of the main findings and theories about the general conditions under which effects have been observed to occur. We call it a psychological model because it deals with mental states and behaviour of individuals.

A principal assumption is that television should be treated as a functional equivalent of any other personal experience, act or observation which might have consequences for either learning or acting. Thus, it covers the case where television not only teaches a behaviour, but also serves as a stimulus for putting into effect a behaviour which has been learnt from another source.

The process depicted by the simplified version of the model (Fig. 3.2.1), can be described in the following way. An individual watching a particular television presentation of a behavioural act receives several possible inputs relevant to behaviour. For purposes of the model, the main input is the portrayal of a specified action (TV act). Other inputs are: the degree of excitement, arousal, attractiveness, interest and motivation to act associated with the presentation (collectively named TV arousal) and the alternative actions or forms of behaviour shown by television in the same context (TV alternatives). In addition, we can consider as relevant inputs the consequences of the main action as these may be shown or implied (TV perceived consequences) and the degree to which the portrayal is shown as realistic (TV perceived reality). The central proposition of the model is that a given portrayal of an action is more likely to lead to learning of that action, the more *salient* it is for the individual (i.e. the more psychologically important), the more *arousal* there is and the more *prominent* the action is in the total repertoire of behaviours available to the individual.

Both salience and arousal are *necessary* conditions for learning, without which the process is negated, while prominence is a matter of degree. The supposition of the model in this respect is only that the smaller the repertoire of available acts, that is to say the fewer the alternatives to the specified TV act, the more likely is the latter to be adopted. Finally, we can observe that for a learned act to be actually applied, there must be an opportunity in real life.

The model is given in the form of an 'itinerary' of an individual in time, starting with exposure to a given television portrayal, proceeding through the experience of acting or not acting and returning to a new or repeated television experience. Thus the model stands for one 'loop' in a sequence in which subsequent television experience will be conditioned or modified by earlier viewing and its consequences. In principle, the model portrays the situation of an individual coming to television for the first time, but in the normal case the model relates to one 'moment' amongst others which make up the experience of television.

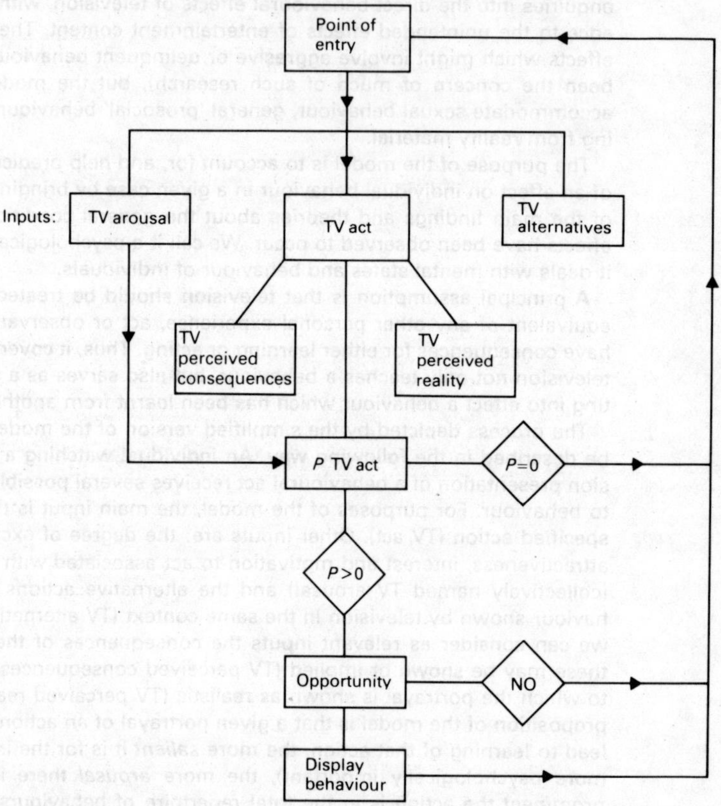

Fig. 3.2.1 A simplified version of Comstock's psychological model of television's effects on individual behaviour (after Comstock et al. 1978).

Definitions of terms in the abridged model

TV act: any form of human behaviour shown on television
Inputs messages from television and associated attributes
TV arousal: extent to which a person is motivated to perform any act in current situation

TV perceived consequences: sum of all positive, minus all negative, values which are learnt from television and which go with a given act
TV perceived reality: degree to which a person perceives the television portrayal (TV act) to be true to life
TV alternatives: other (relevant) social behaviours shown on television
P TV act: probability of carrying out the TV act.
Opportunity: real life chance of putting TV Act into practice
Display behaviour: observable performance of social behaviour shown on television.

Dynamic process of the model

1. An individual observes a television portrayal of a social behaviour, together with associated inputs of arousal, perceived consequences of the behaviour and presentations of other related, similar or alternative behaviours.
2. The probability of any tendency to learn and apply the behaviour depends first on the degree of salience, or psychological importance. According to the thinking underlying the model, an act or behaviour will be given salience firstly, by the demonstration on television, secondly, by the degree of positive value attached to it and, thirdly, by the degree to which it is shown to be close to real life. The authors propose that demonstration on its own will at first increase salience markedly, but after a certain point repeated demonstration will have less and less effect on salience. The values given to an act depend mainly on whether the behaviour is shown to have positive or negative consequences for the actor or for the community. Such valuation will be based on indications of moral justification as well as evidence of personal satisfaction, pain, reward or punishment. The more favourable in value terms is the act, the more salient it tends to be. Reality perception is considered to be very important to the model, since the authors interpret research evidence to show that where portrayals are totally dissociated from real life, the act will have no significance for the individual and produce no tendency to learn or apply. Finally, we can conclude that the degree of salience always depends on the prominence of the given act amongst others and this depends both on the number of other acts presented and the relative time and attention paid to the act in question.
3. At this point in the model we can say that the more salient acts are likely to be adopted and non-salient acts are likely to be ignored. Now the amount of arousal plays a critical part. Arousal comes from two main sources: intrinsic property of the presentation and circumstances of viewing and predisposition of the viewer. These are hard to separate empirically, so that it is proposed only that without some arousal of either kind even salient events will have no effect (*P* TV act = 0). Any increment in arousal will increase the probability of a salient act being applied.
4. For acts which emerge with some probability of application, there must still be some opportunity for trial and where none exists, the process is stopped and the viewer 'returns' to the 'loop' of repeated or further viewing.

5. Finally, there can be implementation of the act itself which is open to observation and the viewer is 'returned' to subsequent viewing experiences in a different frame of mind and with altered probabilities for future behaviour.

Examples

We can describe two hypothetical cases to illustrate the model, one in which behaviour was learned and applied and another in which no observable consequences ensued.

In the first example a viewer sees a realistic police story in which the police hero deals brutally with a drug dealer. A physical beating is shown centrally and realistically in an exciting way and the story suggests that it is a justifiable and necessary, even if illegal, way to deal with someone who would otherwise go unpunished. The salience of the act (the beating) is high, alternatives are not shown and there is an opportunity soon after for a given viewer to act roughly in play with friends. From the model, such action would be predicted, since a positive value is given to aggression under conditions favourable to its learning and application in real life.

In the second hypothetical case, a cartoon film shows a witch poisoning a beautiful and good princess. The degree of arousal is high, but the salience of the poisoning act is low, firstly because the episode is unrealistic and secondly because it is an act with evil consequences carried out by an unattractive actor and perhaps, additionally, because the cartoon is full of violent but unlikely incidents (large repertoire). The question of opportunity does not arise since the probability of imitation is already zero.

Comment

Comstock et al. tested this model against research evidence relating to aggression, pro-social behaviour, political socialization and erotic arousal, mainly derived from studies of children and adolescents. While the model provided a useful framework it was concluded that at many points the model raises more questions than it answers and there was insufficient evidence either to validate or to reject it. There are obvious weaknesses in a model which abstracts one small part of experience from a large and complex web and which tries to subsume many variables under labels which do not have a precise single meaning. However, in order to carry out experimental research in the psychology of the effect process, some abstraction is unavoidable. The model well represents a certain way of doing research according to a particular definition of effects and it could help to clarify thinking which underlines these kinds of research.

Reference

Comstock, G., Chaffee, S., Katzman, N., McCombs, M. and **Roberts, D.** (1978) *Television and Human Behaviour*. New York: Columbia University Press.

3.3 KATZ AND LAZARSFELD'S TWO-STEP FLOW MODEL OF MASS MEDIA AND PERSONAL INFLUENCE

This model emerged originally from the first rigorous study of the effects of mass communication in an election campaign – the United States presidential election of 1940 (Lazarsfeld, Berelson and Gaudet 1944). It was formulated only after further research based on the conclusions of that study. The earlier work was planned implicitly on the basis of a widely current view that the mass media operated according to the classic stimulus-response principles as described in 3.1 above.

The 1940 research showed the inadequacy of this model and of its assumptions. It seemed that aggregate effects from the media were minimal and that this model was unable to represent adequately the social reality of a mass audience, or the process of political information and opinion formation. In assessing the results of the research, the authors revised the model and introduced the idea of a 'two-step flow' of communication and the concept of 'opinion leaders'. Their findings about the relative failure of mass media compared to influence from personal contact led to the suggestion that 'ideas often flow *from* radio and print *to* the opinion leaders and *from* them to the less active section of the population'.

This perception was followed up by more focussed research and by a theoretical re-evaluation of the original model in the book *Personal Influence* by Katz and Lazarsfeld (1955). The two-step flow model, as shown in Fig. 3.3.1 can be more fully characterized according to a number of the findings of this latter work.

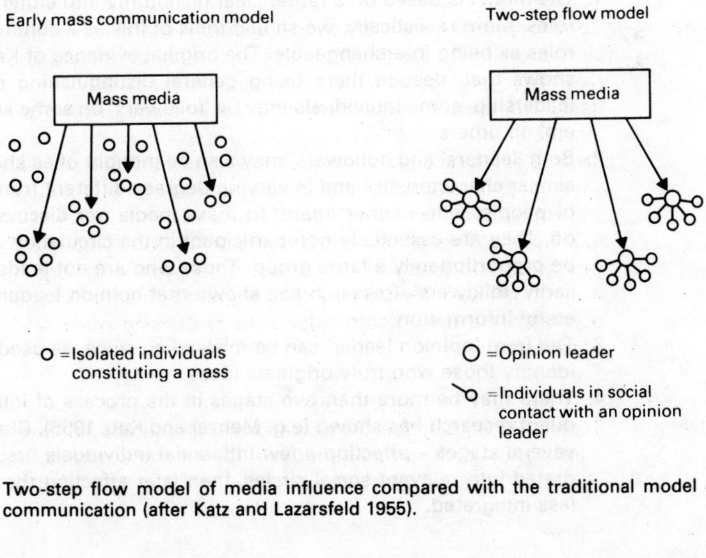

Fig. 3.3.1 Two-step flow model of media influence compared with the traditional model of mass communication (after Katz and Lazarsfeld 1955).

The revised model and research linked to it involves the following main assumptions:

That individuals are not social isolates, but members of social groups in interaction with other people.

That response and reaction to a media message will not be direct and immediate, but mediated through, and influenced by, these social relationships.

That two processes are involved, one of reception and attention and another of response in the form of acceptance or rejection of the influence or information attempt. Reception does not equal response, nor does non-reception equal non-response (because of secondary acceptance from personal contacts).

That individuals are not all equal in the face of media campaigns, but have different roles in the communication process and, in particular, can be divided into those who are active in receiving and passing on ideas from the media and those who mainly rely on other personal contacts as their guides.

That the occupants of the more active role (opinion leaders) are characterized by more use of the mass media, higher levels of gregariousness, a self-perception as influential on others and as having an attributed role as source and guide.

To summarize, according to this model, mass media do not operate in a social vacuum but have an input into a very complex web of social relationships and compete with other sources of idea, knowledge and power.

Comment While communication research has profited greatly from this more realistic version of the mass communication process, the model has proved to be in some respects incomplete and in others potentially misleading. The following points summarize the main lines of criticism.

1. The model is based on a rather clear dichotomy into either active or passive roles. More realistically, we should think of this as a continuum and think of roles as being interchangeable. The original evidence of Katz and Lazarsfeld shows that, despite there being general distinguishing marks of opinion leadership, some individuals may be 'followers' on some subjects and 'leaders' on others.
2. Both 'leaders' and 'followers' may also be thought of as sharing the same or similar characteristics and in varying degrees different from a third category of people, who neither attend to mass media nor discuss with those who do. They are essentially non-participant in the circulation of ideas and may be proportionately a large group. Those who are not leaders are not necessarily 'followers'. Research has shown that opinion leaders are also receivers of information.
3. The term 'opinion leader' can be misleading since, as used here, it does not identify those who truly originate ideas.
4. There may be more than two stages in the process of influence, as subsequent research has shown (e.g. Menzel and Katz 1955). Change can occur in several stages – affecting a few influential individuals first, then those integrated into relevant social circles, then later affecting the more isolated or less integrated.

5. Influence *can* still be direct from the media to the individuals exposed and it is not necessary for the opinion-leader stage to be gone through.
6. The model assumes a situation where mass media channels are the primary or only source of ideas of information. It may be that non-media channels provide the primary source of ideas of knowledge (e.g. work organizations, local political or economic experience). The situation of direct contact between A and B roles, in the Westley MacLean model (2.5 above) represents this circumstance.
7. The model is most appropriate to a developed society under normal social conditions. It would apply less to a traditional society with few media, or to circumstances of crisis and uncertainty in developed societies. In either circumstances there is likely to be a longer relay of contact for passing information and influence from person to person. The idea of a chain of contact is more appropriate than the cluster represented in Fig. 3.3.1.

References

Lazarsfeld, P.F., **Berelson, B.** and **Gaudet, H.** (1944) *The Peoples Choice*. New York: Columbia Univertity Press.

Katz, E. and **Lazarsfeld, P.F.** (1955) *Personal Influence*. Glencoe: Free Press.

Menzel, H. and **Katz, E.** (1955) 'Social relations and innovation in the medical profession', *Public Opinion Quarterly, 19: 337–52.*

3.4 ROGERS AND SHOEMAKER'S MODEL OF INNOVATION DIFFUSION

One of the most important applications of mass communication and research has been concerned with the process of encouraging the adoption of innovations. This is relevant both to developing and to more advanced societies, since there is a continuing need, under conditions of social and technological change, to replace old methods by new techniques. It concerns mass communication, since there are many circumstances where potential changes originate in scientific research and public policy which, to be effective, have to be applied by many individuals or small organizations which are outside the direct centralized control of government or large undertakings.

In practice, the target for most efforts at innovation diffusion have been farmers and members of rural populations. These efforts were first made and evaluated in the United States in the 1920s and 1930s, and are now a feature of most programmes for development in Third World countries. They relate not only to agriculture, but also to health and social and political life. Well before the ideas of interpersonal influence had been formulated and tested in mass communication research (see 3.3), they had been recognized and put into practice by rural sociologists and change agents (Katz 1960).

For the student of mass communication models, the most important features about work on diffusion are: the weight which has to be given to non-media (often personal) sources (neighbours, experts, etc.); the existence often of a campaign situation in which behavioural changes are sought by giving information and trying to influence motivations and attitudes. Because of the large amount of empirical research on diffusion (much of it summarized in Rogers and Shoemaker 1973), the model which has emerged is a much tested one, although it is limited to a set of rather specific circumstances.

The model chosen to illustrate this approach (Fig. 3.4.1) is taken from Rogers and Shoemaker (1973) and is based on the assumption that there are at least four distinct steps in an 'innovation-diffusion' process:

Knowledge: the individual is exposed to an awareness of the existence of the innovation and gains some understanding of how it functions.

Persuasion: the individual forms a favourable or unfavourable attitude towards the innovation.

Decision: the individual engages in activities which lead to a choice to adopt or reject the innovation.

Confirmation: the individual seeks reinforcement for the innovation decision he has made, but he may reverse his previous decision if exposed to conflicting messages about the innovation.

This model incorporates the following ideas about the diffusion process:

(a) Firstly, it distinguishes the three main stages of the whole event into *antecedents, process* and *consequences*. The first of these refers to those circumstances of the event or characteristics of the people involved which makes it more or less likely that an individual will either be exposed to in-

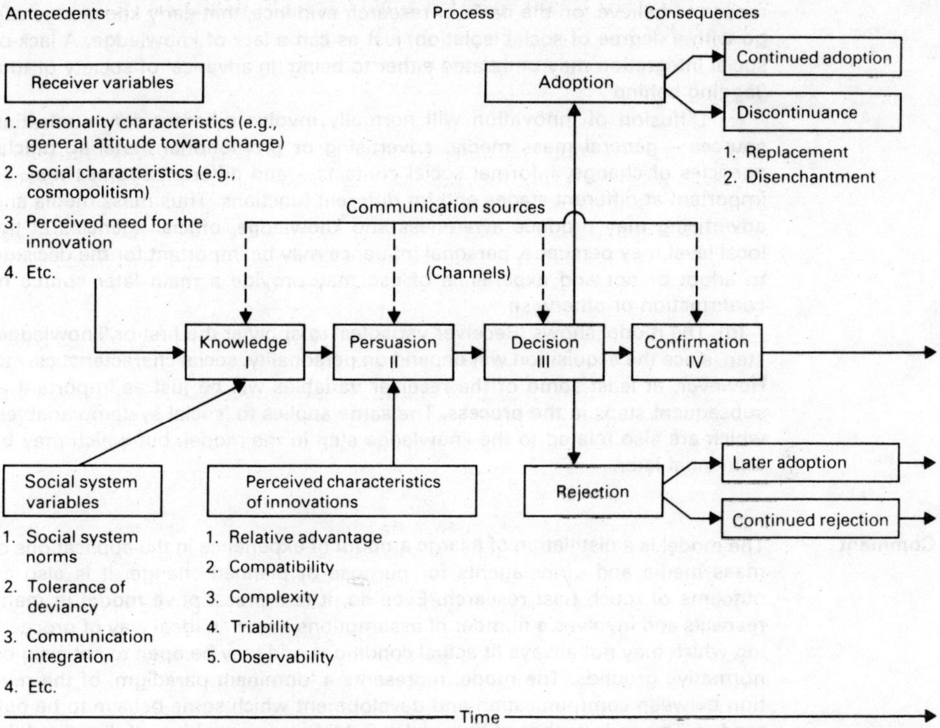

Fig. 3.4.1 **Rogers and Shoemaker's paradigm of the innovation-decision process, indicating the four steps of knowledge, persuasion, decision and confirmation (after Rogers and Shoemaker 1973).**

formation about an innovation or will experience needs to which the information is relevant. For instance, innovation adoption is more likely to occur amongst those who are well-disposed towards change, appreciate the need for innovation and who look out for new information. The *process* is one of learning, attitude change and decision. Here the perceived characteristics of the innovation play a major part, as do the norms and values of the relevant social system. Sometimes technically efficacious means may be unacceptable on moral or cultural grounds or may present a threat to the existing structure of social relations. The stage of *consequences* of the diffusion event is mainly taken to refer to the later history of use or disuse, if adoption takes place.

(b) There is a need to separate out the distinct functions of 'knowledge' 'persuasion', 'decision' and 'confirmation', which must normally occur in this sequence, even if the sequence need not be completed. Different kinds of communication process may also be involved in each case. For instance, the characteristics associated with early persuasibility or persuasiveness. The early knowers are not necessarily the opinion leaders and indeed there is some reason to believe, on the basis of research evidence, that early knowledge can go with a degree of social isolation, just as can a lack of knowledge. A lack of social integration may be related either to being 'in advance' of society or to a 'lagging behind'.

(c) Diffusion of innovation will normally involve different communication sources – general mass media, advertising or promotional material, official agencies of change, informal social contacts – and different sources may be important at different stages and for different functions. Thus mass media and advertising may produce awareness and knowledge, official agencies at the local level may persuade, personal influence may be important for the decision to adopt or not and experience of use may provide a main later source of confirmation or otherwise.

(d) The model shows 'Receiver variables' to apply at the first or 'knowledge' step, since the acquisition will depend on personality, social characteristics, etc. However, at least some of the receiver variables will be just as important at subsequent steps in the process. The same applies to 'social system variables' which are also related to the knowledge step in the model, but which may be influential later.

Comment

The model is a distillation of a large amount of experience in the applications of mass media and other agents for purpose of planned change. It is also an outcome of much past research. Even so, it is a prescriptive model in many respects and involves a number of assumptions about an ideal way of proceeding which may not always fit actual conditions and may be open to criticism on normative grounds. The model represents a 'dominant paradigm' of the relation between communication and development which some believe to be outmoded. The main author of the model, E. M. Rogers, has himself described the passing of this dominant paradigm (Rogers 1976) and has criticisms of the approach which are consistent with some of our comments.

1. The model is designed from the perspective of an external or superior agent of change, which decides what is beneficial (on technical grounds) and proceeds to promote it by mobilizing large resources. Against this, it can be said that change can and should occur from *below* by those who need it on their own behalf. The more this is done, the less relevant is the model presented.
2. The model presupposes a linear, rational sequence of events, planned in advance and with criteria of rationality determined externally. This is a common correlate of the external or manipulative approach just mentioned.
3. In the model, persuasion or attitude change is located between 'knowledge' and 'decision'. This need not necessarily be the case. There are other bases for decision-making than the formation of a judgemental attitude and there is much debate about the notion that attitude change normally precedes a related behaviour change. Often the latter is itself a major *cause* of attitude adjustment.
4. In real life there is much randomness and many elements of chance in decision-making. It is possible that an innovation may be adopted with little knowledge or for prestige, or in imitation of another, etc.

5. The model would be more complete if it included certain feedback loops from later to earlier steps. Thus decision-making and confirmation feedback to knowledge and attitude can increase or reinforce these respectively.

Despite these criticisms, and even because of them, the model is useful and we only want to emphasize that it is not a complete or unique paradigm for the innovation-diffusion process.

References

Katz, E. (1960) 'Communication research and the image of society', *American Journal of Sociology*, **65**: 435–40.

Rogers, E.M. (1976) 'Communication and development: the passing of a dominant paradigm', *Communication Research*, **3**: 213–40.

Rogers, E.M. and **Shoemaker, F.** (1973) *Communication of Innovations*. Glencoe: Free Press.

3.5 NEWS DIFFUSION: THE J-CURVE MODEL

The models dealt with in this chapter have, up to now, been mainly concerned with influence on attitude and behaviour, whether intended or unintended. It should be recalled that a good deal of communication content can be considered as potentially informative rather than persuasive. The purpose of this section is to consider the part played by interpersonal channels in the transmission of news and information by way of mass media.

Much attention was given to the role of person-to-person news diffusion immediately following the Kennedy assassination in 1963 (e.g. Greenberg 1964; Schramm 1971) because of a special concern with the need to control public reaction and avoid panic. There had already been research into the sources of knowledge of news events (Larsen and Hill 1954; Deutschman and Danielson 1960) with particular reference to comparisons between the mass media and personal contacts. The model discussed here grew out of this earlier work, but comes most directly from Greenberg's work on the Kennedy assassination. The J-curve (Fig. 3.5.1) which was used to illustrate and summarize the findings of research is not itself a model but it reflects the outcome of a particular process which can be put into model form (Fig. 3.5.2).

Greenberg set out to test a proposition, based on the earlier work, to the effect that events reported in the news can be classified into three groups, according to the degree of personal diffusion they are likely to receive:

Type I: Events which are of low general importance, but of great significance to a few. Such events will not get prominent treatment in media, but since knowledge of the events is important to a certain target or reference group, they are likely to be selectively noticed by some of the relevant minority and news of them passed on to others who did not happen to see the first announcement. Ultimately, all or most of the relevant group are likely to have some knowledge of the events, but a rather high proportion will have heard through a personal intermediary. An example might be the press publication of national examination results, where the relevant public consists mainly of friends and relatives of the candidates.

Type II: Events which are agreed to be of general public importance (the normal main news stories of the day), which get a fair degree of prominence in the media and are noticed directly by a majority or large minority of the general public. Such stories are not likely to be passed on as information from person to person (although they might be discussed), partly because they can be assumed to be known, partly because they are not usually sufficiently dramatic or immediate to merit personal volunteering of the fact to some other person. Such events might include the settlement of a major strike, a planned rise in train fares, a large bank robbery, a terrorist outrage somewhere else in the world, etc.

Type III: Events of extreme urgency, importance and high dramatic quality which are sure eventually to come to the attention of almost everyone and which get very high and rapid media attention. The classic case is the Kennedy assassination itself. Paradoxically, however, despite the enormous media attention, we can expect the *proportion* of those eventually having the information who heard it first from another person will actually be a good deal higher than in the previous category of main news stories. The significance of the event mobilizes both interpersonal and media communication channels.

The J-curve illustrated in Fig. 3.5.1 is a summary of the results obtained by Greenberg when he investigated the first sources of knowledge of 18 different news events, which ranged in degree of eventual total diffusion from 14 to 100 per cent. When the proportion of people ultimately aware of these events was plotted against the proportion who heard about them first from interpersonal sources, it was possible to group them into five categories (labelled A–E). The resulting curve took on a J-shape in accordance with the proposition outlined below.

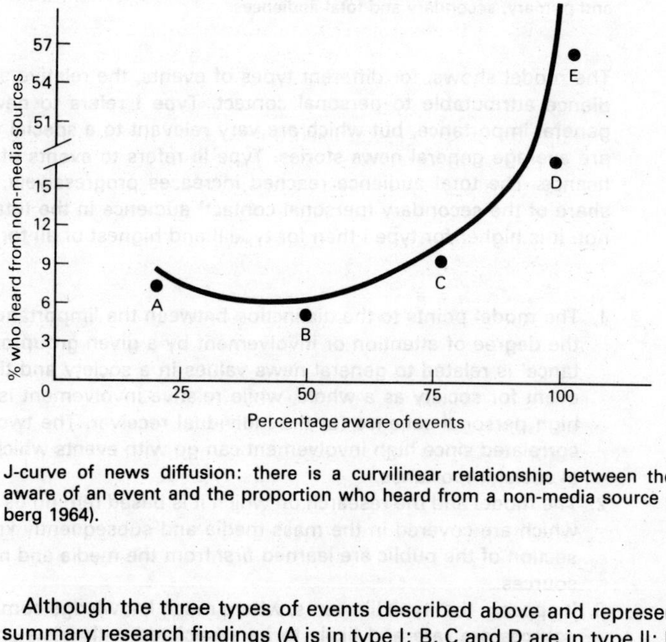

Fig. 3.5.1 J-curve of news diffusion: there is a curvilinear relationship between the proportion aware of an event and the proportion who heard from a non-media source (after Greenberg 1964).

Although the three types of events described above and represented in the summary research findings (A is in type I; B, C and D are in type II; E is in type III) were in ascending order of actual diffusion, as plotted along the horizontal axis, the proportion who heard from personal sources (vertical axis) does not increase progressively and is not related in a linear way. The proportion hearing from personal sources is *rather low* for events of low total awareness, *very low* for most events of 'medium awareness' and then very high (50% +) for events of maximum awareness.

The underlying process which produces this J-shape can be expressed in Fig. 3.5.2.

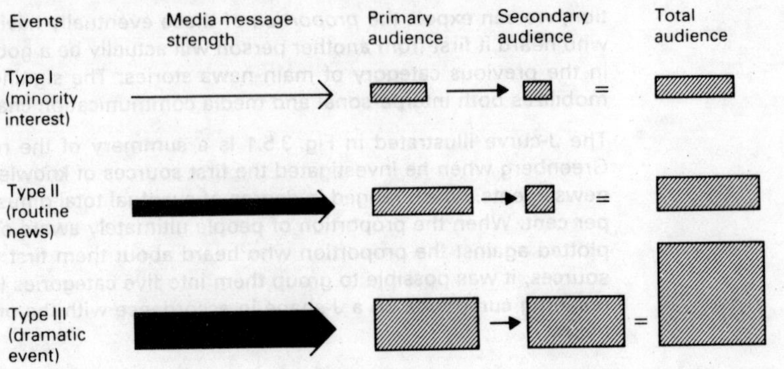

Fig. 3.5.2 Diffusion model underlying the J-curve, showing the relationship between types of event and primary, secondary and total audiences.

The model shows, for different types of events, the relative share of total audience attributable to personal contact. Type I refers to news items of low general importance, but which are very relevant to a special minority. Type II are average general news stories. Type III refers to events of very high significance. The total audience reached increases progressively, but the relative share of the secondary (personal contact) audience in the total audience does not. It is higher for type I than for type II and highest of all for type III.

Comment

1. The model points to the distinction between the 'importance' of events and the degree of attention or involvement by a given group of people. 'Importance' is related to general news values in a society and the salience of an event for society as a whole, while relative involvement is associated with high personal salience for the individual receiver. The two are not directly correlated since high involvement can go with events which have no general social importance.
2. The model and the research on which it is based remind us that *most* events which are covered in the mass media and subsequently known about by a section of the public are learned *first* from the media and not from personal sources.
3. It appears that type III events, where much knowledge comes from personal sources are rare and likely to be associated with crisis situations. We can name as a further distinguishing feature of such events, that they are also likely to be very *rapidly* diffused and come to a *maximum* awareness more quickly than other news events come to *partial* awareness.
4. We know from studies of crisis and rumour (e.g. Shibutani 1966) that the processes outlined by the model can be influenced by unusual conditions, especially conditions of deprivation or attenuation of media sources, in which uncertainty leads to much more active seeking for information from non-media sources.

5. The model lends itself to a wider application than the situation discussed here, since it could help to distinguish between news events of different kinds (e.g. sports results, foreign stories, political events) and between different minority publics amongst the general audience.

References

Deutschmann, P.J. and **Danielson, W.A.** (1960) 'Diffusion of knowledge of a major news story', *Journalism Quarterly*, **37**: 345–55.

Greenberg, B.S. (1964) 'Person-to-person communication in the diffusion of news events', *Journalism Quarterly*, **41**: 489–94.

Greenberg, B. S. and **Parker, E.B.** (eds) (1965) *The Kennedy Assassination and the American Public.* Stanford: Stanford University Press.

Larsen, O. and **Hill, R.J.** (1954) 'Mass media and interpersonal communication in the diffusion of a news event', *American Sociological Review*, **19**: 426–33.

Schramm, W. (1971) in Schramm, W. and Roberts, D. (eds), *The Process and Effects of Mass Communication.* Urbana: University of Illinois Press.

Shibutani, T. (1966) *Improvised News.* New York: Bobbs Merrill.

4 EFFECTS OF MASS COMMUNICATION ON CULTURE AND SOCIETY

4.1 MODELS OF INDIRECT AND LONGER-TERM EFFECTS

During more than a generation of active research into the effects of mass media, there have, inevitably, been important developments in thinking about the effect process. Here we deal with processes which go beyond those envisaged in DeFleur's 'psychodynamic' model (3.1 above), although we should note that DeFleur (1966) had already taken the process somewhat further by speaking of a 'cultural norms' theory of media effect. According to this theory, the media do not only act directly on individuals, but also affect the culture, the stock of knowledge, the norms and values of a society. They make available a set of images, ideas and evaluations from which audience members can draw in choosing their own lines of behaviour.

For example, in the sphere of personal sexual behaviour, the mass media provide cumulatively and often unintentionally a view of what is normal and of what is approved or disapproved. This view may then be incorporated by individuals into their own conceptions of what is either normal or correct. As another example of influence on a social attitude, the mass media seem to provide, on matters of race relations, a relatively homogeneous 'definition of the situation' or statement of the 'problem' and an impression of majority opinion which then helps to shape the response of individuals to specific questions and events (cf. Hartmann and Husband 1974).

The transition in thought represented by the difference between a psychodynamic model on the one hand and a cultural norms theory on the other, corresponds quite closely to the distinction between the models discussed in the last chapter and those which follow in this. Until now, the effect processes we have dealt with have exhibited one or more of the following characteristics: the effects are mainly those intended by the senders; they are short term (i.e. immediate and temporary); they have to do with attitudinal, informational or behavioural changes in individuals; they are relatively unmediated. In general, such effects are relevant to the idea of a 'campaign' – the conscious or planned effort to use publicity for motivational or informational purposes. In some cases, however, as with Comstock (3.2), learning theory or campaign thinking is applied to questions of unintended influence.

In this chapter, by contrast, we are predominantly concerned with effect processes which tend to have the reverse characteristics. That is, they relate mainly to influence which is long term, unplanned, indirect and collective rather than individual in its incidence. In addition, our attention is directed not at separate 'messages', but at whole sets or systems of messages which have similar features. We refer mainly to such matters as: the informal learning of social roles

or norms (socialization); the transmission and reinforcement of basic social values; the tendency for media to convey implicit ideology; the formation of climates of opinion; the differential distribution of knowledge in society; long term changes in culture, institutions and even social structure. As a final remark, we may note that the models of effect to be discussed derive mainly from questions which relate to the 'receiving end' of communication, rather than questions asked by the communicator who has an interest in achieving or avoiding certain consequences.

References

DeFleur, M.L. (1966) *Theories of Mass Communication*. New York: David McKay.

Hartmann, P. and **Husband C.** (1974) *Mass Media and Racism*. London: Davis Poynter.

4.2 AGENDA-SETTING

Amongst the several hypotheses about the effects of mass communication, one that has survived and even flourished in recent years, has held that the mass media simply by the fact of paying attention to some issues and neglecting others will have an effect on public opinion. People will tend to know about those things which the mass media deal with and adopt the order of priority assigned to different issues.

This hypothesis would seem to have escaped the doubts which early empirical research cast on almost any notion of powerful mass media effects, mainly because it deals primarily with learning and not with attitude change or directly with opinion change. Empirical studies of mass communication had in fact confirmed that the most likely effects to occur would be on matters of information. The agenda-setting hypothesis offers a way of connecting this finding with the possibility of opinion effects, since what is basically proposed is a learning function from the media. People learn what the issues are and how they are ordered in importance.

The best known of the more recent proponents of the agenda-setting hypothesis are the American researchers Malcolm McCombs and Donald Shaw (1972, 1976). They wrote (1976) 'Audiences not only learn about public issues and other matters through the media, they also learn how much importance to attach to an issue or topic from the emphasis the mass media place upon it. For example, in reflecting what candidates are saying during a campaign, the mass media apparently determine the important issues. In other words, the mass media set the "agenda" of the campaign. This ability to affect cognitive change among individuals is one of the most important aspects of the power of mass communication.'

It has been the case that most 'agenda-setting' research has concerned itself with election campaigns. In the typical modern election campaign it has become a common strategy to establish the 'image' of a given candidate by association with certain positions on the perennial problems of a society and with certain special issues of the candidate's choice. The theory is that if voters can be convinced that an issue is important, they will vote for the candidate or party which has been projected as most competent to deal with it.

In addition to its relevance for the practice of political campaigning, the hypothesis has the advantage of appealing to common sense and of seeming relatively easy to test. As shown in Fig. 4.2.1, the basic idea is that, amongst a given range of issues or topics, those which get more media attention will grow in their familiarity and perceived importance over a period of time, and those which get less will decline correspondingly. It should be possible to test this expectation by comparing the results of quantitative media content analysis with changes in public opinion as measured by surveys at two or more points in time.

McCombs and Shaw (1976) take the Watergate affair as an illustration of the agenda-setting function. There was nothing new in uncovering political corruption, but the intense press exposure and the televised US senate hearings that

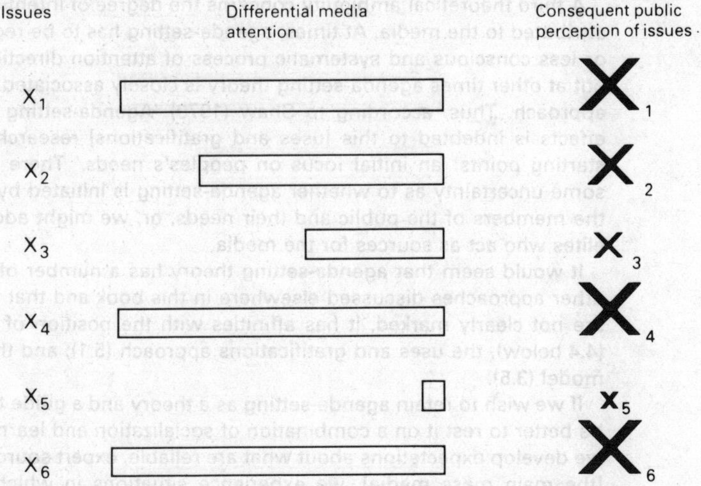

Fig. 4.2.1 The agenda-setting model: matters given most attention in the media will be perceived as the most important.

followed, made it the topic of the year. Nevertheless, the detailed evidence from research has not always confirmed the existence of a powerful agenda-setting process. The authors of the model report some confirmatory evidence, but others (e.g. McLeod et al. 1974) warn against an 'uncritical acceptance of agenda-setting as a broad and unqualified media effect'.

Comment Some of the uncertainty about the hypothesis stems from unresolved problems in the underlying theory. It is not, for example, always clear whether we should look for direct effects from the media on the personal agendas of individual members of the audience or whether we can expect agenda-setting to work through interpersonal influence. This makes quite a lot of difference to research and to the extent to which we can rely on content analysis to provide an indication in itself of likely agenda-setting effects.

A second problem has to do with the different kind of agendas which are involved. We can speak of the agendas of individuals and groups or we can speak of the agendas of institutions – political parties and governments. There is an important distinction between the notion of setting personal agendas by communication directly to the public and of setting an institutional agenda by influencing the politicians and decision makers. We can expect the media to have a multiple role in that they may try to influence the opinion of the public and they may also try to influence the élite. In reality there is a continuous interaction between élite proposals and public views, with the media acting as carrier as well as source (see Fig. 2.4.2.)

A third theoretical ambiguity concerns the degree of intention which may be attributed to the media. At times, agenda-setting has to be regarded as a more or less conscious and systematic process of attention directing by the media, but at other times agenda-setting theory is closely associated with a functional approach. Thus, according to Shaw (1979) 'Agenda-setting theory of media effects is indebted to this [uses and gratifications] research tradition for its starting points: an initial focus on peoples's needs.' There is, consequently, some uncertainty as to whether agenda-setting is initiated by the media or by the members of the public and their needs, or, we might add, by institutional élites who act as sources for the media.

It would seem that agenda-setting theory has a number of boundaries with other approaches discussed elsewhere in this book and that these boundaries are not clearly marked. It has affinities with the position of Noelle-Neumann (4.4 below), the uses and gratifications approach (5.1), and the news diffusion model (3.5).

If we wish to retain agenda-setting as a theory and a guide to research it may be better to rest it on a combination of socialization and learning theory. Thus, we develop expectations about what are reliable, expert sources of information (the main mass media), we experience situations in which knowledge and judgement about public matters is expected of us and we acquire the means to meet these expectations by learning from the media.

References

McCleod, J.M., **Becker, L.B.** and **Byrnes, J.E.** (1974) 'Another look at the agenda setting function of the press', *Communication Research*, **1,2**: 131–66.

McCombs, M. E. and **Shaw, D.L.** (1972) 'The agenda setting function of mass media', *Public Opinion Quarterly*, **36**: 176–87.

McCombs, M.E. and **Shaw, D.L.** (1976) 'Structuring the 'Unseen Environment', *Journal of Communication*, Spring: 18–22.

Shaw, E.F. (1979) 'Agenda-setting and mass communication theory', *Gazette*, xxv, **2**: 96–105.

4.3 BALL-ROKEACH AND DEFLEUR'S DEPENDENCY MODEL OF MASS COMMUNICATION EFFECTS

This model, described by Ball-Rokeach and DeFleur (1976), has as its principal focus the structural conditions of a society which govern the likelihood of occurrence of effects from the mass media. Basically, it is a social structural model which has its origins in ideas about the nature of a modern (or mass) society in which the mass media can be considered as 'information systems vitally involved in maintenance, change and conflict processes at the societal as well as the group and individual levels of social action'. (See Fig. 4.3.1.)

Perhaps the most important and original idea expressed by the model is that in modern societies audience members come to depend on mass media information resources for their knowledge of, and orientation to, what is happening in their own society. The kind and degree of dependency will depend on a number of structural conditions, but the most important of these relate, firstly, to the degree to which the society is subject to change, conflict or instability and, secondly, to the degree that the mass media do, in fact, serve many unique and central information functions. The model consequently shows the interrelation between three main sets of variables and specifies the main kinds of effects which are dependent on the interaction of these three.

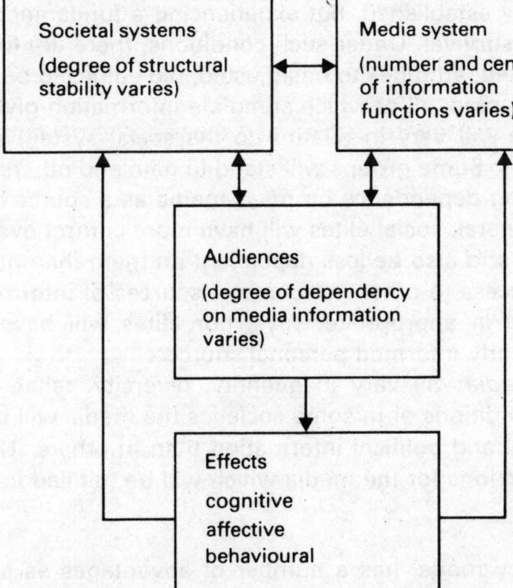

Fig. 4.3.1 Ball-Rokeach and DeFleur's dependency model, showing the interdependence between society, mass media, audience and effects (after Ball-Rokeach and DeFleur 1976).

The discussion which accompanies the model specifies some of the effects which might be usefully studied by this approach. These can be summarized as follows:

(a) *Cognitive*
Creation and resolution of ambiguity
Attitude formation
Agenda-setting
Expansion of peoples' belief systems
Value clarification

(b) *Affective*
Creating fear, anxiety
Increasing or decreasing morale (alienation)

(c) *Behavioural*
Activation or de-activation
Issue formation or issue resolution
Reaching, or providing, strategies for action (e.g. political demonstration)
Causing altruistic behaviour (e.g. donating money to charities)

In interpreting the model, it is important to bear in mind that the three main components of audience, media system and social system are all interrelated, although the nature of this relationship varies from one society to another (see 6.1 below). Each component can also vary in ways which are directly relevant to the differential occurrence of effects:

The social system varies according to its degree of stability. It may be firmly established but going through some temporary crisis, or, as with some developing countries, it may be in a condition of rapid change. Alternatively, it may be strongly established, but experiencing a fundamental challenge to its legitimacy and survival. Under such conditions, there are likely to be new objects to be defined, attitudes to be adjusted, old values to be reasserted or new ones to be promoted, all of which stimulate information-giving and -receiving.

The audience will vary in relation to the social system and to changes in social conditions. Some groups will stand to gain and others to lose. There will also be a varying dependence on mass media as a source of information and guidance. In general, social élites will have more control over the media, more access to them and also be less dependent on them than non-élites. They will tend to have access to other more expert sources of information. Unless specially organized in appropriate ways, non-élites will have to rely on mass media or on poorly informed personal sources.

The mass media will vary in quantity, diversity, reliability and authority. Under some conditions or in some societies the media will be more central for providing social and political information than in others. There can also be a diversity of functions for the media which will be fulfilled in varying degrees.

Comment The dependency model has a number of advantages as an approach to the study of general media effects.

1. It is open to a wide range of effect possibilities, as has been indicated. The authors themselves claim that it 'avoids a seemingly untenable all-or-none position of saying either that the media have no significant impact on peo-

ple or society, or that the media have an unbounded capacity to manipulate people and society'. We may refer to this as a 'contingency' model, in the sense that any given effect is dependent on a more or less unique set of circumstances which hold in a given situation.

2. It directs attention to structural conditions and historical circumstances rather than to individual and personality variables. It is thus more suitable for dealing with sociological questions than most other overall communication models.
3. It takes account of the fact that effects on the audience may also lead to effects on the social system and on the media system itself. Thus it can happen that experience of media performance may lead to demands for change or reform of the media, to be carried out either through the political system, or by the free market mechanism, by the emergence of alternative media.

A weakness of the model is that it overstates the real independence of the different elements and especially of the media system from the social system. The former tends to be presented as if it were a neutral 'non-political' source available to meet whatever 'need' might arise. It is more likely that a media system will be quite closely associated with, or even incorporated into the dominant institutions of society.

Reference **Ball-Rokeach, S.** and **DeFleur, M.L.** (1976) 'A dependency model of mass media effects', *Communication Research*, **3**: 3–21.

4.4 THE SPIRAL OF SILENCE

This model deals with the question of how public opinion is formed. Professor Elisabeth Noelle-Neumann (1974), a German sociologist, argues in her model – the 'spiral of silence' – that the answer to this question lies in an interplay between mass communication, interpersonal communication and the individual's perception of his own opinion in relation to others in society.

The model rests in part on earlier social psychological thinking (e.g. Allport 1937), to the effect that one's own opinion is to a very large degree dependent, upon what others think or, rather, upon what one perceives as the opinion of others.

An essential idea underlying this model, illustrated in Fig. 4.4.1, is that most individuals try to avoid isolation in terms of being alone in holding certain attitudes and beliefs. Therefore one observes one's environment in order to learn which views are prevailing or gaining strength and which are less dominant or declining. If one believes that one's own views are among those in the latter category, one will be less inclined to express them, just because of the fear of isolation.

And so, the dominant or gaining opinion tends to be even more so:

> The more individuals perceive these tendencies and adapt their views accordingly, the more the one faction appears to dominate and the other to be on the downgrade. Thus the tendency of the one to speak up and the other to be silent starts off a spiraling process which increasingly establishes one opinion as the prevailing one. (Noelle-Neumann 1974)

The perception of the individual is, of course, not the only force working in this model. Mass media are another. What is the dominant view of the day is often

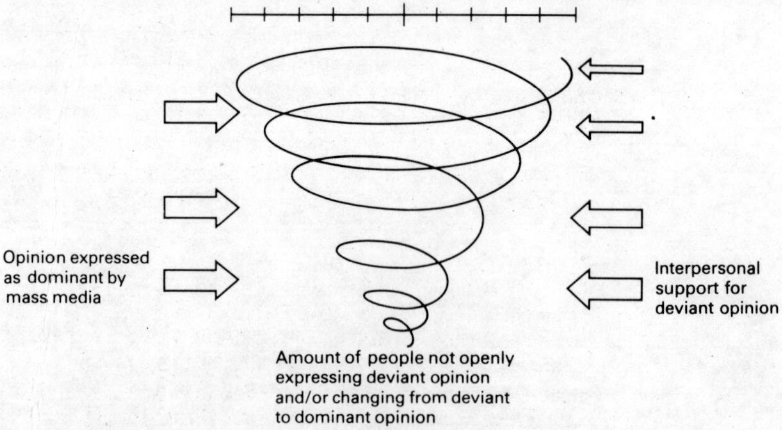

Fig. 4.4.1 An example of a spiral of silence: mass media expressing dominant opinion together with an increasing lack of interpersonal support for deviant views bring about a spiral of silence, with an increasing number of individuals either expressing the dominant opinion or failing to express deviant ones (after Noelle-Neumann 1974).

defined by the media. Another 'force' working in the process is the degree of support from people in one's environment. As one remains silent oneself other people around will do so as well, and so mass media definitions and lack of expressed support for one's own views in interpersonal communication bring about the spiral.

Noelle-Neumann has supported her model by reference to changes over time in several important areas of public opinion in the German Federal Republic (e.g. Noelle-Neumann, 1980). Her evidence strongly indicates a relationship between perceptions of majority opinion, expressions of personal opinion, tendencies in content and the opinions of journalists. Under some conditions, the mass media appear to mould perceptions of the dominant opinion and thus influence individual opinions in the way proposed by the model.

Comment

The ideas expressed in this model are not in themselves new, although they have been brought together in a new way and given a new relevance to conditions of widespread reliance on television as a main source of information and ideas. We can recognise earlier theories about the consequence of communication monopoly and we are familiar, from election studies, with the possibilities of 'band-wagon' effects. Another relevant concept in this connection is that of 'pluralistic ignorance' (Scheff, 1967) which refers to situations in which many individuals fail to communicate private opinions to each other and come to feel that they belong to a dissenting minority. In fact, a majority may privately hold the same view, while allowing a powerful and vocal minority to impose a false consensus. The idea of a 'silent majority' refers to a similar phenomenon.

One interesting question about the model is whether or not the spiral represents real attitude change or not. It may be that only the *expression* of ideas assumed to be deviant is hampered and that under more favourable conditions these opinions could rather quickly and unexpectedly reappear. The answer will partly depend on the definition of public opinion used, since for Noelle-Neumann free expression is an essential part of the concept of public opinion. In the nature of things, it is extremely difficult to obtain satisfactory empirical confirmation of the theory and the hardest and most controversial part of any confirmation procedure has to do with the question of media consonance and cumulation in respect of given opinion matters. It would require an elaborate and extensive analysis of media content to deal satisfactorily with this problem. The process of opinion forming represented by the model almost certainly occurs under some conditions and to some degree, but the extent of its occurrence is still not known.

References

Allport, F.H. (1937) 'Towards a science of public opinion', *Public Opinion Quarterly*, **1**: 7–23.

Noelle-Neumann, E. (1974) 'The spiral of silence: a theory of public opinion', *Journal of Communication*, **24**: 43–51.

Noelle-Neumann, E. (1980) 'Mass media and social change in developed societies' in Wilhoit, G.C. and de Bock, H. (eds), *Mass Communication Review Yearbook*, pp. 657–78. Beverly Hills: Sage Publications.

Scheff, T.J. (1967) 'Towards a sociological model of consensus', *American Sociological Review*, **32**: 32–46.

4.5 INFORMATION GAPS AS EFFECTS

In considering long-term effects of mass communication it is important to take into account the discussion of so-called knowledge or information gaps. A background to this discussion is formed by the steadily increasing flow of information, to a large degree made possible by mass media. This increase ought, theoretically speaking, to benefit everyone in society since every individual gets a possibility of finding his bearings in the world around him and may, perhaps, more easily enlarge his horizons.

However, several researchers have lately pointed out that the increased flow of information often has the negative effect of increasing knowledge within certain groups far more than in others, and that *'information gaps'* will occur and increase, i.e. the distance between one social group and another in knowledge about a given subject.

The knowledge gap hypothesis

An early contribution in this field is the knowledge gap hypothesis of Tichenor et al. (1970). It claims that when the flow of information in a social system is increased, the better educated, those with a higher socio-economic status, will be able to absorb the information better than less educated people with lower status. Increased information thus results in widening the knowledge gap instead of diminishing it.

Rogers (1976) points out that information results not only in increasing *knowledge* gaps, but also in gaps concerning behaviour and attitudes. Accordingly, he changes the term to 'the communication effects gap'. He also remarks that mass communication is not the only cause of the gaps. Communication directly between individuals may also have similar effects. He finally underlines the fact that the gaps need not be caused exclusively by different levels of education – other factors may also contribute to the creation of such gaps.

Communication potential

A Swedish research group has built a discussion around the term 'communication potential' (see Nowak et al. 1976 and Fig. 4.5.1). The term stands for those characteristics and resources which enable the individual to give and take information, and which facilitate the communication process for him. In this discussion, the communication potential is regarded as a means of obtaining certain values in life:

The size and shape of the communication potential depends on three main types of characteristics or resources:

(a) Personal characteristics. Man has both certain basic, often native *faculties*, like seeing and speaking, and acquired *abilities*, like speaking different

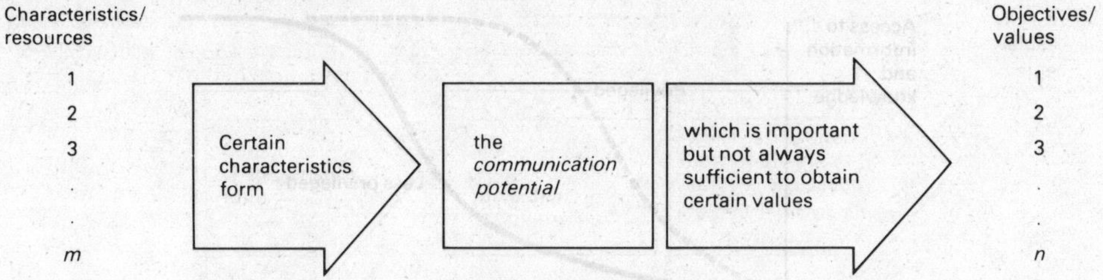
Characteristics/
resources
1
2
3
.
.
m
Certain
characteristics
form
the
communication
potential
which is important
but not always
sufficient to obtain
certain values
Objectives/
values
1
2
3
.
.
n

Fig. 4.5.1 The communication potential decides whether or not an individual will attain certain values. (After Nowak et al, 1976)

languages and typewriting. Besides, he has a potential for communication, knowledge, attitudes, and traits of personality.

(b) Characteristics dependent on the individual's social position. This position is defined by variables like income, education, age, and sex.

(c) Characteristics of the social structure in which the individual is found. An important factor is the functioning of the individual's primary groups (e.g. family, working group), and his secondary groups (e.g. clubs, associations, school, organizations) when it comes to communication. In this context, society as a communication system is also relevant.

The potential may lead to the individual's obtaining certain values and reaching certain objectives. As examples of such values, the authors mention the experiencing of a sense of identity and solidarity, being able to affect one's life situation, and being able to affect society as a whole.

If we regard the above model as a model of mass media, we should consider the three types of characteristics (or resources) as independent (causal) variables. The degree of achievement of one's objectives and values then become a dependent variable (effect or consequence). In a broader perspective, we may assume the following: If, in a society, there are systematic differences between the communication potentials of different groups, this will result in systematic differences in the achievement of objectives and values of the respective groups.

From 'a gap' to 'gaps'

The phenomenon in question has been often talked about as 'the information gap' or 'the knowledge gap' in society. This is certainly an over-simplification. There exists not only one information gap, but many, and they do not look alike. It is conceivable that the information gap or knowledge gap concerning world politics is wider than that concerning the increased costs of foodstuffs during the past few years. Taking our point of departure from the various information gaps in a particular society, we would also find that the different gaps cut through the population in different ways.

It is often claimed that the gaps tend to increase as time passes. This may be true in some cases, but Thunberg et al. (1979) consider that they often acquire the aspect as shown in Fig. 4.5.2.

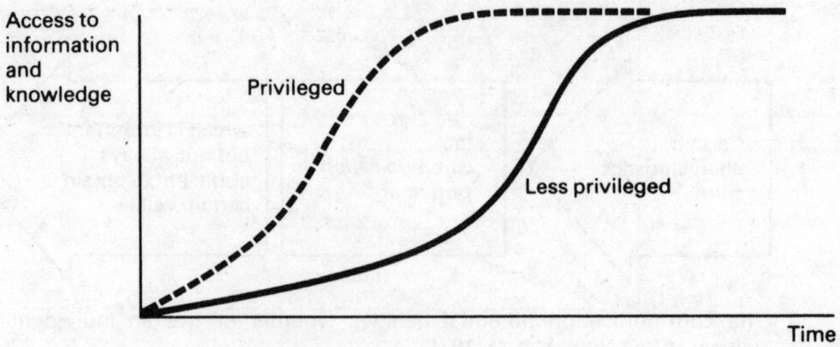

Fig. 4.5.2 Closing information gap, in which the less privileged group 'catches up' with the more privileged one (after Thunberg et al. 1979).

In this figure, the dotted line represents the readings-off relevant to those groups in society which are privileged in respect of communication, i.e. those with a high communication potential. The continuous line represents the corresponding development in less privileged groups. We see how the gap is at first increased, but how the less privileged category 'catches up' with the other. The final result is that the information gap is closed, as far as this particular subject goes. As an example we may consider the information campaign which preceded the change in Sweden from left-hand over to right-hand traffic. At the outset there was, to be sure, a certain information gap or knowledge gap, which later disappeared.

Some researchers term this phenomenon of the two curves approaching and joining 'ceiling effects'. Such ceilings may be reached when the potential information about the subject in question is limited. Those who have a large capacity for absorbing information after some time have no more to gather from the information flow on a particular subject. This fact enables the less privileged to catch up. It is also conceivable that a ceiling is reached when the privileged group in a certain situation no longer feels motivated for seeking more information, while the less privileged group is still motivated and in the long run becomes equally well informed (see Ettema and Kline 1977).

The American researchers Donohue et al. (1975) exemplify the failure of many gaps to close with reference to knowledge of space research and of the smoking and cancer issue. In both cases, the authors maintain, heavy media attention resulted in widened gaps between higher and lower educated categories. It is also conceivable that, when a subject drops out of the general discussion, so that nobody or very few talk about it any longer, the gap between privileged and underprivileged remains or may even widen. Such a development is illustrated in Fig. 4.5.3.

Comment In a dynamic society, new information gaps appear incessantly, as various subjects increase and decrease in topicality and relevance. The conditions favourable or unfavourable to each gap vary, depending on the complexity or content of the subject. The communication potential mentioned above should, however, be a decisive factor, according to Nowak et al. (1976). This is especially

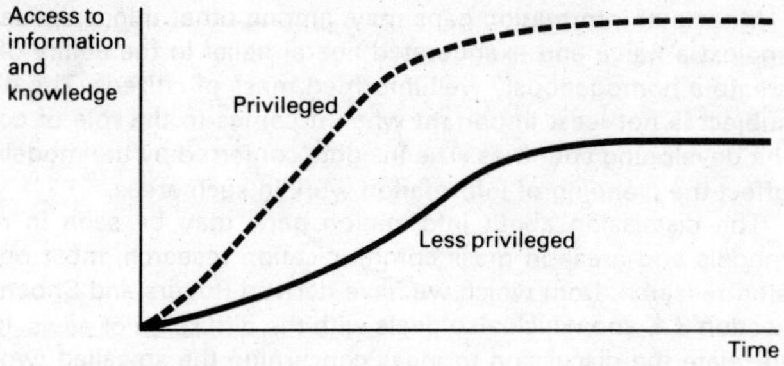

Fig. 4.5.3 Non-closing information gap (after Thunberg et al. 1979).

relevant to subjects about which it is 'profitable' to be well-informed. If we are to regard the information gaps in a sociological light, the important thing is not the amount of information as such, but *what* information one is able to absorb (and transmit).

The actual development of different information gaps depends on many factors. Donohue et al. (1975) proposed, for example, the following hypotheses which received support:

1. Where an issue arouses general concern for a community as a whole, knowledge about that issue is more likely to become more evenly distributed.
2. This equalization is more likely to occur when the issue emerges in a climate of social conflict.
3. Such equalization in knowledge is more likely to occur in a small, homogenous community than in a large, pluralistic one.

The opinion of Rogers (1976) cited above that mass media are not the only creators of information gaps, is relevant here. In many cases, such gaps may appear because communication between individuals works better with some categories of people than with others. In one well-known American investigation, for instance, it was found that doctors who had good contact with their colleagues and frequently communicated with them, were quicker to accept new medical discoveries than doctors who were more isolated.

It is an interesting question whether different media tend to create different types of gaps. There is some evidence that television has got a greater potential for closing gaps than has the press. This may be due to the fact that TV usually is a more homogenous and limited source, whereas in the case of the press, each paper reaches different publics with a more differentiated content. Probably more significant is the fact that television is a widely trusted source and tends to reach a higher proportion of the public, in many countries, with public affairs information.

New media such as various forms of televised data transmission, where information is individually distributed, may also have a tendency to widen information gaps since their use will depend on the individual's interests, motivation and previous knowledge and such media are more available to better-educated and higher-status groups.

Models of information gaps may, among other things, be seen as a reaction against a naive and exaggerated liberal belief in the ability of mass media to create a homogenously well-informed mass of citizens. The discussion of this subject is not least important when it comes to the role of communication in the developing countries. The insights conferred by the models may decisively affect the planning of information work in such areas.

The discussion about information gaps may be seen in relation to other models and areas in mass communication research, most obviously to diffusion research, from which we have derived Rogers and Shoemaker's model in section 3.4, and which also deals with the diffussion of news. It is also possible to relate the discussion to ideas concerning the so-called two-step flow of information hypothesis (3.3) and to the dependency model (4.3).

References

Donohue, G.A, Tichenor, P.J. and **Olien, C.N.** (1975) 'Mass media and the knowledge gap', *Communication Research*, **2**: 3–23.

Ettema, J.S. and **Kline, F.G.** (1977) 'Deficits, differences and ceilings: contingent conditions for understanding the knowledge gap', *Communication Research*, **4**: 179–202.

Nowak, K., Rosengren, K.E. and **Sigurd, B.** (1976) 'Kommunikation, underprivligiering, mänskliga värden' in *Kommunikation, Social Organisation, Mänskliga Resurser*, Samarbetskommittén för Långtidsmotiverad Forskning, Stockholm.

Rogers, E.M. (1976) 'Communication and development: the passing of the dominant paradigm', *Communication Research*, **3**: 213–40.

Tichenor, P.J. Donohue, G.A. and **Olien, C.N.** (1970) 'Mass media and differential growth in knowledge', *Public Opinion Quarterly*, **34**: 158–70.

Thunberg, A.M., Nowak, K. and **Rosengren, K.E.** (1979) *Samverkansspiralen*. Stockholm: Liber Förlag.

5 AUDIENCE-CENTRED MODELS

5.1 THE USES AND GRATIFICATIONS APPROACH

As we already pointed out, much of the history of mass communication research has dealt with effects, with media influence on people. The catchphrase associated with the so-called 'uses and gratifications approach' captures the main difference between this approach and traditional effects research: instead of studying what the media do with people, let us study what people do with the media.

Research within this tradition focusses on the *uses* of media content for obtaining *gratifications* or need fulfillment. Audience behaviour is to a large extent to be explained by the *needs* and *interests* of the individual. It is important to underline that this is a model of the *receiving* process and that it does not embrace the whole communication process.

McQuail (1979) has mentioned two main impulses behind the emergence of the 'uses' approach. Firstly, there was the opposition to deterministic assumptions about media effects. This was a part of the 'rediscovery of people' (Katz and Lazarsfeld 1955), occurring especially in American sociology. Secondly, there was a wish to break out of a rather sterile debate over mass media taste. In this matter, the uses and gratifications approach provided an alternative way of looking at the relation between media content and the audience, and of categorizing media content – according to 'function' rather than 'level of taste'.

Uses and gratifications research may be divided into a 'classical' and a 'modern' period (Höst 1979). The former included studies such as that of Herzog (1944) which dealt with gratifications sought and obtained by listeners to radio soap operas and Suchman's (1942) study of motives for listening to classical music on radio. To these may be added Berelson's (1949) study of what readers of New York dailies said they missed most during a newspaper strike.

In the 1960s and 1970s research into media uses and gratifications appeared in more elaborate forms – the 'modern' studies of which some will be mentioned later on.

One may argue about whether there is *one* single uses and gratifications model or a number of them, but there certainly is some agreement among the researchers as to the main idea. Katz et al. (1974) describe the underlying logic of investigations into media uses and gratifications as follows: 'They are concerned with (1) the social and psychological origins of (2) needs, which generate (3) expectations of (4) the mass media or other sources, which leads to (5) differential patterns of media exposure (or engagement in other activities), resulting in (6) need gratification and (7) other consequences, perhaps mostly unintended ones.' We can put this in model form in Fig. 5.1.1

In addition to the key element above, gratifications research models often

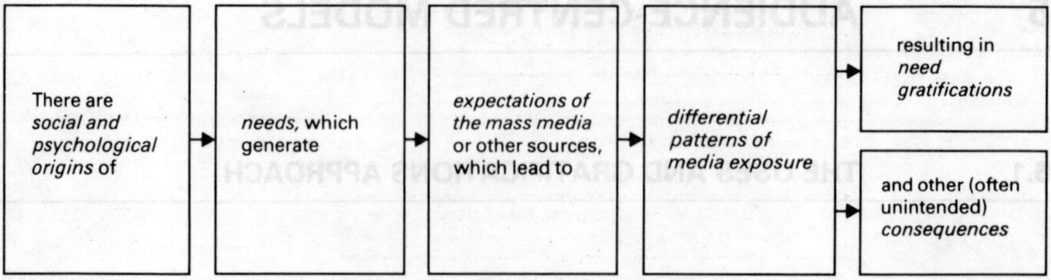
There are
social and
psychological
origins of
needs, which
generate
expectations of
the mass media
or other sources,
which lead to
differential
patterns of
media exposure
resulting in
need
gratifications
and other (often
unintended)
consequences

Fig. 5.1.1 The elements of a uses and gratifications research model.

include *motives* for satisfying needs and *functional alternatives* for fulfilling the needs. As for the latter, a certain type of media consumption may be a functional alternative to, for example, other types of cultural activity.

An example of a typical uses and gratifications way of reasoning might go as follows: a certain individual has, like most human beings, a basic need for social interaction. From experience, he expects that a certain mass media consumption or use will give him some fulfillment of this need. This leads him to watch certain TV programmes, read certain types of magazine content, etc. In some cases this results in need gratification, but it may equally result in dependence on mass media and in changed habits. In the case described we may say that his mass media use serves as a functional alternative to real interaction.

Rosengren's version

Among the single models within their particular field, perhaps the most widely cited is that of Rosengren (1974). It takes into account most of the elements and relations relevant to the approach. Eleven elements are related to each other as shown in Fig. 5.1.2.

The needs of the individual constitute the starting point. The development of need does not, of course, occur in a vacuum but in interaction with elements within and around the individual (boxes two and three). With a reference to Maslow's (1954) hierachy of needs, Rosengren claims that the higher level needs (the need for company, love, acceptance and self-actualization) are those of most relevance for the uses and gratifications models, compared to the lower level needs (psychological and safety needs).

In box four, the author introduces the concept of problems, which are created by the interaction of needs, individual characteristics and surrounding social conditions. 'Problems' and 'needs' should not be confused, although they often are, Rosengren remarks. The salience of these problems differs between individuals, and this is also the case with the perceptions of how the problems may be solved (box five).

On the individual level, perceived problems and their solutions may give *motive* for action (box six). 'Motive' may be difficult to separate from 'need'

1. Certain basic human needs of lower and higher order — under interaction with
2. Differential combinations of intra- and extra-individual characteristics — and also with
3. The structure of the surrounding society, including media structure — result in
4. Differential combinations of individual problems, being more or less strongly felt, — as well as
5. Perceived solutions to these problems, — the combination of problems and solutions constituting
6. Differential motives for attempts at gratification- seeking or problem-solving behaviour, — resulting in
7. Differential patterns of actual media consumption — and
8. Differential patterns of other behaviour, — both behaviour categories giving
9. Differential patterns of gratifications or non-gratifications — and, possibly, affecting
10. The individual's combination of intra- and extra-individual characteristics — as well as, ultimately,
11. The media structure and other social, political, cultural and economic structures in society.

Fig. 5.1.2 Rosengren's uses and gratifications paradigm (after Rosengren 1974).

and 'problem', especially in empirical research. The motives may be directed towards a wide range of goals of gratification or problem solving types.

Research provides some examples: certain social situations are experienced as so laden with conflict and tension that individuals acquire motives for relaxation through media consumption (Katz and Foulkes 1962). The individual may be aware of problems in society and is thus motivated to seek information for further orientation in the media content (Edelstein 1973). Individuals lacking possibilities to fulfill their need for interaction in a 'natural way' are consequently motivated to use certain types of media content (e.g. television drama) (Rosengren and Windahl 1972).

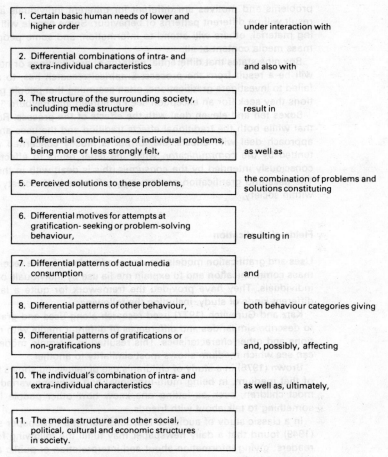

Problems, resulting in motives will, thus, cause action either in the form of media consumption or in other behaviour (boxes seven and eight). As needs, problems and motives are different for different individuals and groups, the result will be different patterns of behaviour. Some people will seek entertaining material, others will attend to information, and some people will not use mass media content at all.

Box nine states that differential patterns of gratifications or non-gratifications will be a result from the process. Empirical research has, to a large degree, failed to investigate gratifications, often assuming that people get the gratifications they seek (for an exception see Palmgreen and Rayburn 1979).

Boxes ten and eleven deal with the effects of the process. Rosengren notes that while both the traditional effects tradition and the uses and gratifications approach deal with effects, the former is mostly concerned with effects intended by the *communicator*, while the latter refers to effects more or less consciously intended by the *consumer* (this is dealt with in the next section). The uses and gratification process may influence both society and the media within society.

Fields of application

Uses and gratification models are designed to describe the receiving process in mass communication and to explain media use by individuals or aggregates of individuals. They have provided the framework for quite a large number of different kinds of study, including the following:

Katz and Gurevitch (1977) used research along uses and gratifications lines to describe similarities and differences of different media with respect to functions and other characteristics. This resulted in a simple model in which one can see which medium shows most similarity to another.

Brown (1976) in a study of children's use of television shows the importance of that medium, in being multi-functional and in giving varied satisfaction to most children, such as letting one know how other people live and giving something to talk about with friends.

In a classic study of audience reactions during a newspaper strike, Berelson (1949) found that a daily newspaper may fulfill the following functions for its readers: giving information about and interpretation of public affairs; being a tool for daily living and a source of respite; giving social prestige; giving social contact; and being used as a part of the daily ritual.

Comment

The uses and gratifications approach has been the target for much criticism. Some of the objections may be summarized like this:

1. The approach is often said to be too individualistic in method and conception. This makes it difficult to tie to larger social structures.
2. The empirical research relies to a high degree on subjective reports of mental states and is hence too 'mentalistic'. Furthermore, some of the psychological elements explaining media use tend to vary in more or less fixed ways with the social position of the individual. Consequently, a model containing variables such as socio-economic status, education etc., might explain as much of mass communication behaviour and gratifications model (cf. Elliott 1974).

3. The uses and gratifications models depict the audience as fairly active – especially in comparison to the audience of the 'mass society model'. Its activity lies in that it selectively and freely chooses among different media contents. The notion of such an active audience may be regarded as inconsistent with another assumption of this approach, namely that motives are determined by basic needs, social experience and conditions. In addition, there is some empirical evidence to show that the television audience, at least, is distinctly unselective (Goodhart, 1975).
4. The approach shows little or no sensitivity to the substance of the media content itself, dealing mainly with very general categories of content.
5. The approach has a functionalistic character. For example, media consumption fills certain functions and is regarded as restoring balance in giving need fulfillment. Criticism of functionalism may, thus, also apply to the uses and gratifications research.
6. The tradition has been charged with other drawbacks: it is said to be conservative in nature and to serve as a pretext for producers of 'bad' content, who may claim that they are just filling the needs of the audience members. In spite of this criticism, the approach has many advocates and has, seemingly, best survived in the United States.

References

Berelson, B. (1949) 'What missing the newspaper means' in Lazarsfeld, P.F. and Stanton, F.N. (eds), *Radio Research 1948–49*. New York: Harper and Brothers.

Blumler, J.G. and **Katz, E.** (eds) (1974) *The Uses of Mass Communications*. Beverly Hills: Sage Publications.

Brown, J.R. (1976) 'Children's use of television' in Brown, J.R. (ed.), *Children and Television*. London: Collier, Macmillan.

Edelstein, A. (1973) 'An alternative approach to the study of source effects in mass communication', *Studies of Broadcasting*, March, **9**: 5–29.

Elliott, P. (1974) 'Uses and gratifications research: a critique and a sociological alternative' in Blumler, J.G. and Katz, E. (eds), *The Uses of Mass Communications*. Beverly Hills: Sage Publications.

Goodhart, G.J., Ehrenberg, A.S.C. and **Collins, M.A.** (1975) *The Television Audience: patterns of viewing*. Farnborough: Saxon house.

Herzog, H. (1944) 'What do we really know about daytime serial listeners?' in Lazarsfeld, P.F. and Stanton, F.N. (eds), *Radio Research*. New York: Duell, Sloan and Pearce.

Höst, S. (1979) 'Moderne bruksstudier – snarvei eller blindspor?' *Institute for Mass Communication Research*, University of Oslo (mimeo).

Katz, E., Blumler, J.G. and **Gurevitch, M.** (1974) 'Utilization of mass communication by the individual' in Blumler, J.G. and Katz, E. (eds), *The Uses of Mass Communications*. Beverly Hills: Sage Publications.

Katz, E. and **Foulkes, D.** (1962) 'On the use of mass media for "escape": clarification of a concept', *Public Opinion Quarterly, 26*.

Katz, E. and **Gurevitch, M.** (1977) *The Secularization of Leisure: culture and communication in Israel*. London: Faber.

Katz, E. and **Lazarsfeld, P.F.** (1955) *Personal Influence*. Glencoe: The Free Press.

Maslow, A.H. (1954) *Motivation and Personality.* New York: Harper and Brothers.

McQuail, D. (1979) 'The uses and gratifications approach: past, troubles and future', *Massacommunicatie*, vii, **3**: 73–89.

Palmgreen P. and **Rayburn, J.D.** (1979) 'Uses and gratifications and exposure to public television, a discrepancy approach', *Communication Research*, **6**: 155–80.

Rosengren K.E. (1974) 'Uses and gratifications: a paradigm outlined' in Blumler, J.G. and Katz, E. (eds), *The Uses of Mass Communications.* Beverly Hills: Sage Publications.

Rosengren, K.E. and **Windahl, S.** (1972) 'Mass media consumption as a functional alternative' in McQuail, D. (ed.), *Sociology of Mass Communications.* Harmondsworth: Penguin.

Suchman, E. (1942) 'An invitation to music' in Lazarsfeld, P.F. and Stanton, F.N. (eds), *Radio Research, 1941.* New York: Duell, Sloan and Pearce.

5.2 A USES AND EFFECTS MODEL

We have already presented both the effects tradition and the uses and gratification approach. It has been noted in both cases that they have been criticized from different points of view. All the same, there is little doubt that each contains a core of viable elements. It is an aim of the model to be discussed here to consider the useful elements of both traditions, leaving what is less good behind.

As the title indicates, the uses and effects model, presented by Windahl in 1979, is a synthesis of uses and gratifications and effects paradigms, a thought that is far from new (cf. for example Klapper 1963).

The concept of 'use'

The concept of 'use' is in this context of great importance and is, so to speak, the heart of the model. Knowledge about media use and of its origins will provide keys for understanding and predicting outcomes of the mass communication process.

'Mass media use' may mean many different things. It may be the same as 'exposure' which merely indicates an act of perceiving. In another context it may stand for a rather complex process, in which a certain content is consumed under certain conditions, fulfilling certain functions and to which are tied certain expectations for gratification. The author of the model finds the latter concept more useful than the former. The mere act of using may be described in terms of the *amount* of content used, the *type* of content used, the *relations* to media used (e.g. identification) and way of using it, for example if the consumption is a primary or secondary activity.

In the uses and gratifications model, media use is basically determined by the basic needs of the individual. In this model (Fig. 5.2.1), need is but one factor leading up to use.

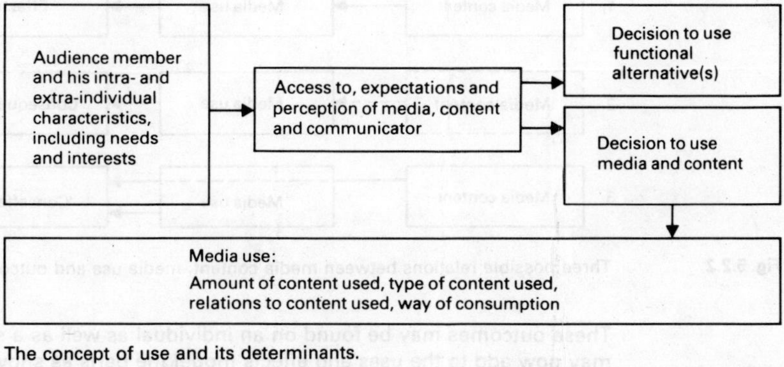

Fig. 5.2.1 The concept of use and its determinants.

Individual characteristics, expectations and perception of media and the degree of access to media will lead to decisions by the individual about whether to use or not to use mass media content. For most media activities there are functional alternatives, e.g. real interaction instead of pseudo-interaction through the TV set.

Effects, consequences and 'coneffects'

The outcomes of the mass communication process and their relations to media use constitute the second important part of the model. The use-outcome relation takes on different shapes (here we also take media content into account):

(a) In most effects models, the characteristics of the media content determine most of the outcomes. Media use may, in such cases, be conceived of as only an intervening factor. The outcome of such a process may be labelled 'effect'. The uses and gratifications process thus serves to mediate, reinforce or to weaken the effects of content.

(b) In many processes, outcomes are more the results of use than of content characteristics. Media use may exclude, prevent or reduce other activities. It may also have psychological consequences such as dependence on specific media. When use is the main cause of the outcome, the latter is labelled a 'consequence'.

(c) One may also think of outcomes, which are partly determined by media content, (mediated by use), partly determined by use itself. There are, thus, two processes working more or less simultaneously, together causing a result that we may call a 'conseffect'. Educational processes often result in such 'conseffects'. Part of the outcome is caused by content encouraging learning (effect), part of it is the result of a process whereby media use leads automatically to some acquisition and storing of knowledge.

These three combinations are visualized in Fig. 5.2.2.

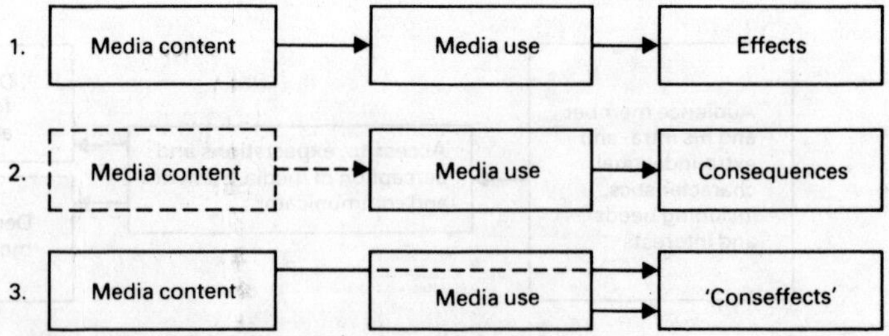

Fig. 5.2.2 Three possible relations between media content, media use and outcomes.

These outcomes may be found on an individual as well as a societal level. We may now add to the uses and effects model the parts as shown in Fig. 5.2.3.

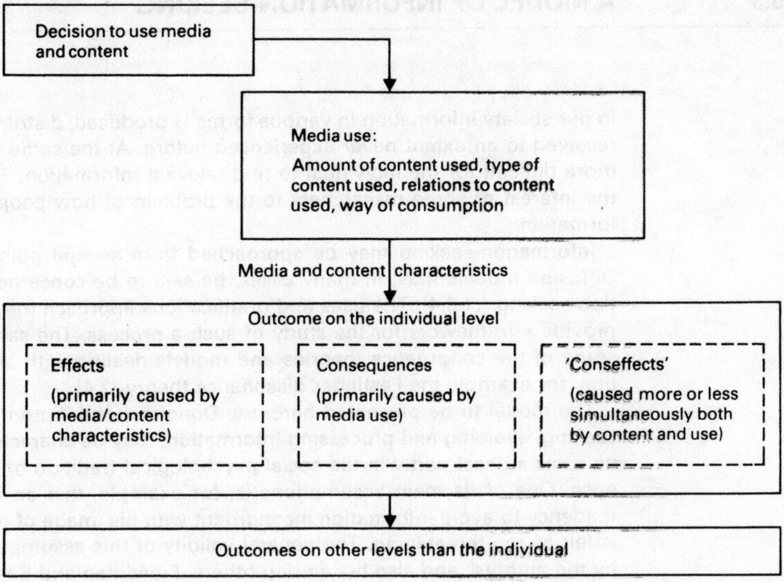

Fig. 5.2.3 The 'use' and the 'outcome' part of the uses and effects model.

Comment This is thus an effort to bring together two major research paradigms, trying to avoid some of the shortcomings of both. In particular it suggests a way of incorporating uses and gratifications thinking into traditional effect models. It has an additional advantage of presenting a defined 'use' concept. It also adds to the possibility of distinguishing analytically between different kinds of outcomes, that is, accordingly to cause or origin of the outcome in question.

On the other hand, one may point to the difficulties in deciding if a certain outcome is an effect, a consequence or a 'conseffect'. Most cases of mass communication outcomes are not as clear-cut as those examples given above.

References Klapper, J. T. (1963) 'Mass communication research: an old road resurveyed', *Public Opinion Quarterly*, **27**: 516–27.

Windahl, S. (1979) 'A uses and effects model: some suggestions', Media Panel Report No 7b. University of Lund (mimeo).

5.3 A MODEL OF INFORMATION-SEEKING

In our society information in various forms is produced, distributed, stored and received to an extent never experienced before. At the same time it becomes more difficult for the individual to find relevant information. This has directed the interest of some researchers to the problem of how people seek their information.

Information-seeking may be approached from several points of departure. Diffusion models may, in many cases, be said to be concerned with information-seeking (cf 3.4). The uses and gratifications approach may also be said to provide a framework for the study of such a process. The same is true about some of the congruence theories and models dealing with attitude organization, for example the Festinger dissonance theory (2.4).

The model to be presented here, the Donohew and Tipton (1973) model of seeking, avoiding and processing information, may be characterized as having its roots at least partly in the social psychological tradition of attitude congruence. One of its main assumptions is, for example, that an individual has a tendency to avoid information incongruent with his image of reality because it is felt as too threatening. The general validity of this assumption is discussed by the authors; and also by, among others, Freedman and Sears (1966).

Before describing the graphic model, some of its key concepts will be considered. We will begin with that of 'image' or 'image of reality'. The image is first of all a result of the individual's lifetime experiences and consists of 'goals, beliefs and knowledge' which he has acquired.

A second part of the image consists of the individual's self-concept, in which is included his evaluation of his ability to handle different situations.

Thirdly, the image of reality consists of an information-using 'set' which rules the individual's behaviour in seeking and processing information

When seeking information, the individual may choose among different strategies. In this model a distinction is made between a broad focus and a narrow focus strategy. In the first case the individual first makes an inventory of possible information sources, reviews it and makes a choice of which source to use.

In the narrow focus strategy, one single source is taken as a point of departure and further seeking is done with this source as a kind of base for the seeking.

In the model, the term 'closure' is used to refer to the point when the information seeker stops seeking more information.

The flow chart

In Fig. 5.3.1 where the model is presented as a flow chart, the process starts as an individual is exposed to a cluster of stimuli. To that he may pay attention or not. Whether he does, depends partly on the characteristics of the stimuli.

At the next stage, a comparison between the stimuli (information) and image of reality held by the individual, takes place. Here, the degree of relevance and of consistency between image and stimuli is checked. Too threatening or non-important material may be screened out at this point as well as stimuli experienced as monotonous because of their high degree of consistency. If stimuli are rejected this may lead to an end of the process ('stop').

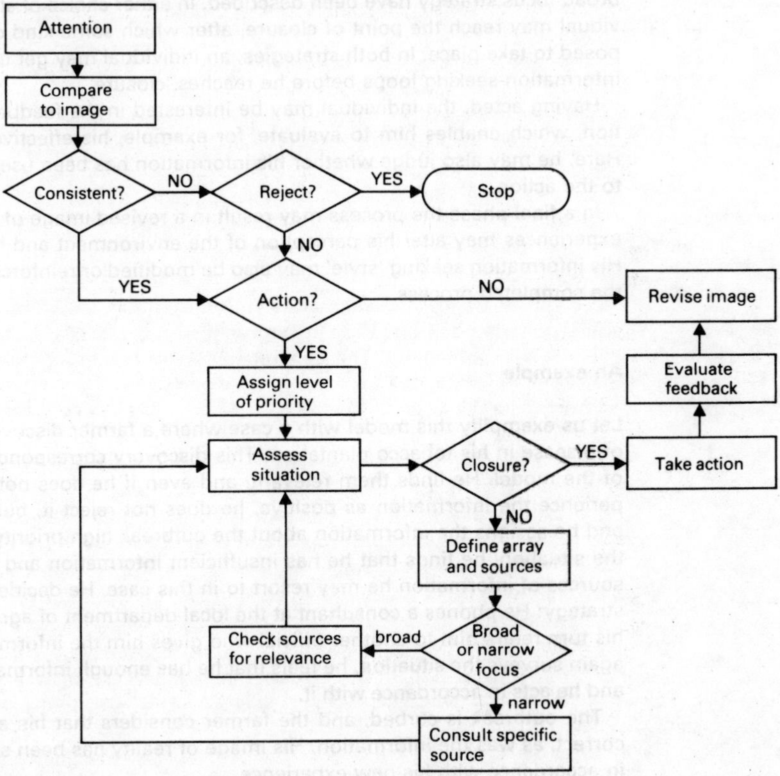

Fig. 5.3.1 Donohew and Tipton's flow chart model of seeking, avoiding and processing information (after Donohew and Tipton 1973).

Next, a question whether the stimuli demand action or not is put forward. If the answer is 'no' the effect of the stimuli may be that they form an additional part of the image.

Properties of the image of reality, such as experience, self-concept and style of information processing determine in part what action is to be taken by someone who gives a positive answer to the 'action question'.

Let us now assume that the individual assigns the stimuli a certain level of priority in comparison to other stimuli. In an assessment of the situation ('what questions do I need to answer?'), the individual may choose either to exert closure (thinking one has enough information) or to seek further information.

In the latter case, the individual will have to define his information needs and assess the potential sources ('Which are the sources I need in order to answer my questions?').

Given more than one potential information source, one has to make up one's mind about what information strategy to choose. Above, the narrow and the broad focus strategy have been described. In either choice of strategy, the individual may reach the point of closure, after which some kind of action is supposed to take place. In both strategies, an individual may get into a number of information-seeking loops before he reaches 'closure'.

Having acted, the individual may be interested in the feedback from the action, which enables him to evaluate, for example, his effectiveness in acting. Here, he may also judge whether his information has been useful and relevant to the action.

In a final phase the process may result in a revised image of reality. His new experiences may alter his perception of the environment and his self-concept. His information seeking 'style' may also be modified or reinforced as a result of the completed process.

An example

Let us exemplify this model with a case where a farmer discovers an outbreak of disease in his tobacco plantation. This discovery corresponds to the stimuli of the model. He finds them relevant, and even if he does not, of course, experience the information as positive, he does not reject it, but decides to act and he assigns the information about the outbreak high priority. On surveying the situation, he finds that he has insufficient information and considers what sources of information he may resort to in this case. He decides on a 'narrow' strategy: He phones a consultant at the local department of agriculture, who in his turn refers him to another official who gives him the information. When he again surveys the situation, he feels that he has enough information ('closure'), and he acts in accordance with it.

The outbreak is curbed, and the farmer considers that his action has been correct, as was the information. His image of reality has been slightly changed in accordance with his new experience.

Comment

It must be noted that the authors themselves describe this model as preliminary and tentative. They stress, for example, that 'the actual order of the steps are somewhat arbitrary'. One may say that its chief merit lies in the fact that it identifies important factors and relationships in the information-seeking process. It also gives a broad perspective in taking into account steps before and after the actual information-seeking.

The process described is mainly intrapersonal and one may criticize it because it does not take into account factors such as the interplay between the information seeker and his environment. The authors themselves remark that factors such as information availability and time limits that have a great predictive value should be accounted for.

As for the use of the model, Donohew et al. (1978) have used it to describe different information seeking styles and to characterize different types of information seekers.

References

Donohew, L. and **Tipton, L.** (1973) 'A conceptual model of information seeking, avoiding and processing' in Clarke, P. (ed.), *New Models for Communication Research*. Beverly Hills: Sage Publications.

Donohew, L., Tipton, L. and **Haney, R.** (1978) 'Analysis of information-seeking strategies', *Journalism Quarterly*, 25–31.

Freedman, J. L. and **Sears, D.** (1966) 'Selective Exposure' in Berkowitz, L. (ed.), *Advances in Experimental Social Psychology*. New York: Academic Press.

6 MASS MEDIA SYSTEMS, PRODUCTION, SELECTION AND FLOW

6.1 COMPARATIVE MEDIA SYSTEMS: A FREE MARKET MODEL AND ITS ALTERNATIVES

Most of the models described so far in this book have been concerned with interpersonal and group processes of communication, although in Chapter 4 the discussion was widened in scope to deal with longer-term processes taking place at the level of society. So far, there has been little attention to formal institutions and organizations which shape mass communication processes – in particular the production and distribution of content. In the present chapter we deal with some aspects of the *mass media institutions* which carry out the work of 'mass communicating'. In doing so, we reach the limit of what can easily be described, since we are faced with complex systems and structures with too many interdependent elements to be easily represented in simple graphic form. Nevertheless, some sub-processes of media institutions which have important consequences for what is actually disseminated to the public have been, or can be, usefully expressed as models. We begin, however, with an overall view of the media system in which we may recognize some of the elements which were introduced in the chapter on basic models, especially those of Westley and McLean (2.5), Riley and Riley (2.7) and Maletzke (2.8).

DeFleur's model of the American mass media system

This model places mass communication in the context of other institutions – especially the political and economic – which directly shape the relationship between communicator, message and public. It refers to the American media system as a whole and was first presented by DeFleur in 1966. The version shown in Fig. 6.1.1 is a much simplified and more schematized version of the original, designed to emphasize the important component elements, which could be found in almost any national system of mass communication. It is necessary to stress that this model represents only a liberal or free market version of the mass media system since, as we see below, any variations in the balance of political and economic forces in a society can have important consequence for the structure and relationships depicted.

The model concentrates on the function of what DeFleur calls 'low-taste' content in the American system. Such content includes by far the greater part of all media output and is exemplified by such categories as 'crime drama, confessional magazines, daytime serials' etc. The evaluative label 'low taste' is used because such content is frequently criticized for its potentially harmful moral

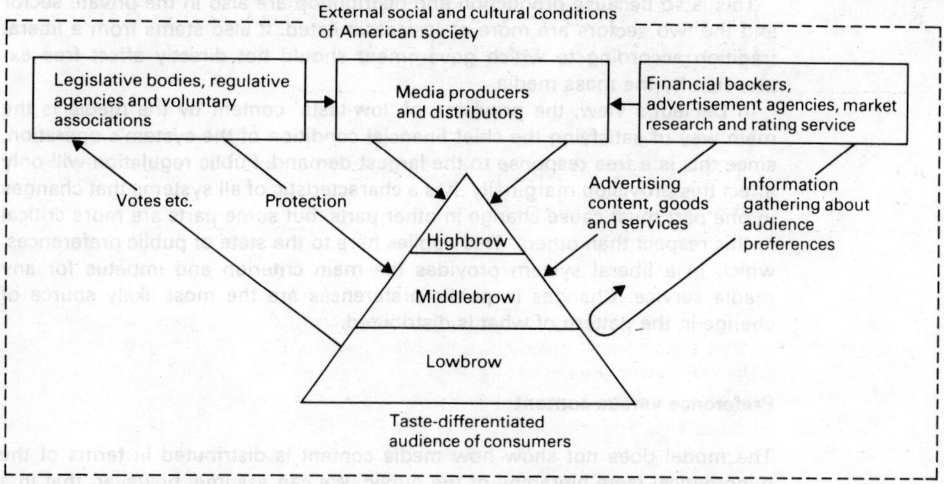

Fig. 6.1.1 DeFleur's model of the American mass media system (after DeFleur 1970).

and social effects and low aesthetic and intellectual quality. The starting point for the analysis is the observation that such content continues to flourish, despite criticism, precisely because its continued existence is a necessary condition for, and an inevitable outcome of, the American system.

The main elements in the model can be described as follows:

Firstly, the audience, differentiated according to a hypothetical distribution of taste or preference levels – high, middle, low.

Secondly, the financial and commercial agencies which provide capital for media production, buy advertising time and space and obtain their own income from other business activities. Such agencies use marketing and survey research so as to match public preferences, audience purchasing power and habits and the interests of advertisers. Their main task, as shown in the model, is to acquire information about audience preferences and provide a very powerful feedback to the producers in the form of financial support.

Thirdly, there are media production and distribution organizations, which, in this case, are mainly private corporations which have to operate profitably in a mass production system.

The fourth element stands for public regulation and control institutions, governmental as well as voluntary which exert pressure of various kinds. Such institutions receive inputs and feedback from the public, sometimes through the political system. Their activities may directly affect producers either through rules about media content or through technical and financial controls applied in the public interest (e.g. control of airspace or monopoly). This element in the model acts to counterbalance the private commercial interest, but the model in Fig. 6.1.1 does not say anything about how well the two sectors do actually balance each other. We may assume from DeFleur's discussion that the private, commercial sector has much greater power over content.

This is so because production and distribution are also in the private sector and the two sectors are more or less assimilated. It also stems from a liberal tradition according to which government should not directly affect free expression by the mass media.

In DeFleur's view, the provision of 'low-taste' content by the media is the main way of satisfying the chief financial condition of the system's operation, since this is a free response to the largest demand. Public regulation will only affect this provision marginally. It is a characteristic of all systems that changes in one part must cause change in other parts, but some parts are more critical in this respect than others. This applies here to the state of public preferences, which in a liberal system provides the main criterion and impetus for any media service. Changes in public preferences are the most likely source of change in the pattern of what is distributed.

Preference versus content

The model does not show how media content is distributed in terms of the hypothetical taste hierarchy of the public. We can assume, however, that in a purely commercial system, the two distributions should coincide very closely, so that audiences 'will get what they want'. Even so, there will be some measure of divergence, of the kind illustrated in Fig. 6.1.2.

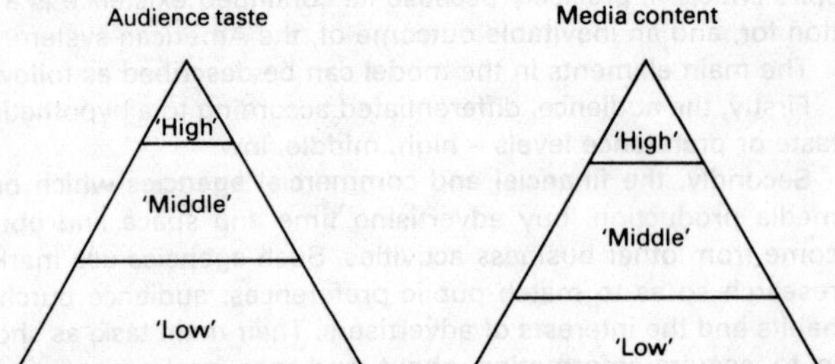

Fig. 6.1.2 Audience preference versus media content structure in the liberal model, showing little difference between the two.

The divergence illustrated indicates an actual supply of 'high-taste' content greater than is justified by the frequency distribution of assumed demand. This 'overrepresentation' has two sources. One is the effect of public and political pressure, and perhaps subsidy, for educational and cultural supply. Another, and more important, cause is the likelihood that 'high-taste' demand comes from a part of the audience with higher purchasing power, who are more interesting to certain kinds of advertiser and more able to pay higher prices for specialized media content corresponding to their 'higher' cultural taste.

Other media systems

While there is a good deal of diversity of media systems in the world we can look briefly at two main types which are alternative to the commercial or liberal model just outlined and open to comparison in some key respects in terms of this model. One can best be called a 'social-responsibility' model and the other labelled Soviet or socialist (see Siebert et al. 1956). In our discussion the former stands for the kind of mixed system which predominates in western Europe, in which there is often a large element of public intervention in broadcasting and also several institutionalized ways of making private media accountable to society.

The model of such a system, by comparison with that of DeFleur would show a larger and more powerful public sector component with a stronger and more direct influence on content. Correlatively, the freedom of producers to respond to commercial demands would be more limited. The lines of feedback from audience to producer would not be so predominantly routed through the commercial agencies. The main probable effect of changing the model in this way would be to reduce the direct power of audience demand to determine supply and to increase the divergence between 'taste' as measured by market research and actual provision. The difference might be of the kind shown in Fig. 6.1.3.

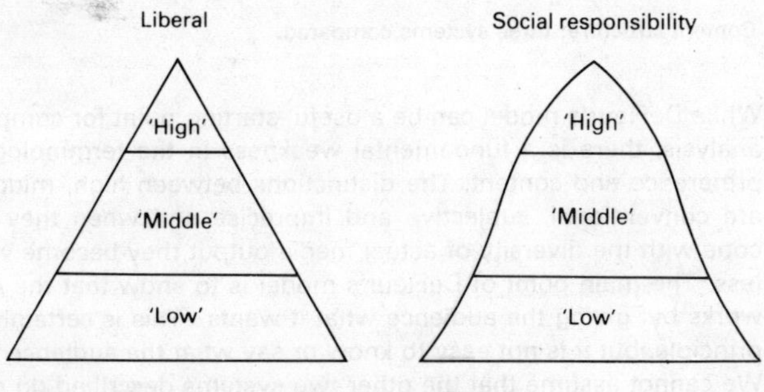

Fig. 6.1.3 Content structure: two systems compared.

A social responsibility system involves stronger requirements on producers to provide information, education and culture and to satisfy minority tastes which might not be commercially viable (here included in the 'high-taste' category). The pressures come from political sources and from cultural élites which tend to have greater power in the societies concerned than they do in the United States.

A Soviet or socialist (East European) model, while differing in several important respects, can be compared with the case shown by DeFleur. There would certainly be a much stronger public regulatory sector and a rather weak commercial sector, involving little more than revenue from direct sales. Whereas in the liberal model production is more or less assimilated by the commercial sector, here the public sector tends to assimilate production. The whole nature of the system will be very different, but again one observable effect is likely to be seen in the distribution of content. The provision would be even less responsive to direct audience consumer demand and more guided by other criteria of selection than in the social responsibility case. Figure 6.1.4 compares hypothetical content distributions of three models.

The depiction is based on the assumption that criteria applied in the socialist model and backed by public power of control will weigh content production even more towards cultural, educational and informational content which would conventionally be classified as 'high taste'.

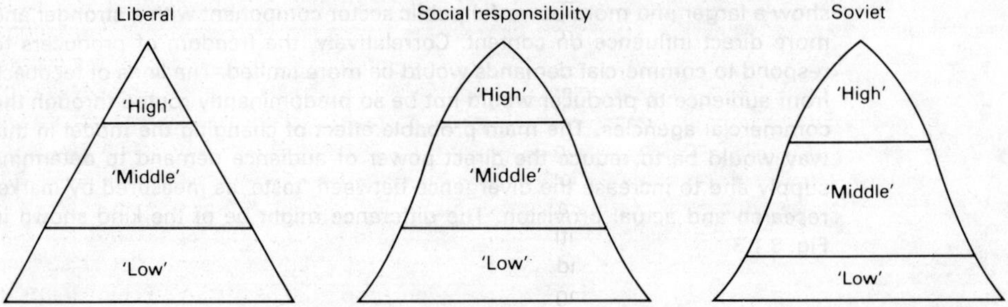

Fig. 6.1.4 Content structure: three systems compared.

Comment While DeFleur's model can be a useful starting point for comparative or critical analysis, there is a fundamental weakness in the terminology for classifying preference and content. The distinctions between high, middle and low taste are conventional, subjective and imprecise and when they are stretched to cope with the diversity of actual media output they become virtually meaningless. The main point of DeFleur's model is to show that the American system works by 'giving the audience what it wants'. This is certainly the free market principle, but it is not easy to know or say what the audience really does want. We cannot assume that the other two systems described do *not* give the audience what it wants, since audience preferences have several levels, overlap, change and resist definition and classification. In addition, the market mechanism is not the only way of assessing what audiences want, like, or find useful and satisfying.

References

DeFleur, M.L. (1966) *Theories of Mass Communication*. New York: David McKay.

Siebert, F.S., Peterson, T. and **Schramm, W.** (1956) *Four Theories of the Press*. Urbana: University of Illinois Press.

6.2 MEDIA ORGANIZATIONS: MASS COMMUNICATOR-PUBLIC RELATIONSHIPS

From the beginning, definitions of mass communication have tended to emphasize the 'distance' between the mass communicator and the audience. The distance was attributed to three main factors: the physical concentration of facilities for production and distribution, usually in metropolitan locations which are not very accessible to most individual members of the public; the use of technologies which mainly allowed only one-directional contact, and thus little feedback from audience to communicators; the cultural and social distances which stem from the usually higher socio-economic, informational and sometimes political status of mass communicators. For some, the separation of media from audience was an inherent limitation which gave mass communication an inevitably undesirable character. Other writers, researchers and communicators have considered this as a practical problem which had to be solved in one way or another if the mass media were to operate effectively and meet the needs of their audience.

One way of dealing with this question is to focus on the relationship between mass communicator and the audience. This section presents not one model but a typology consisting of three alternative models of such relationships between communicator and public. The main question which the typology sheds light on has to do with the different ways in which the distance or gap mentioned at the outset can be bridged or rendered unproblematic under the normal conditions of mass media operation. The three basic types of relationship can be named as a dominance model; an autism model; a balance/exchange-model.

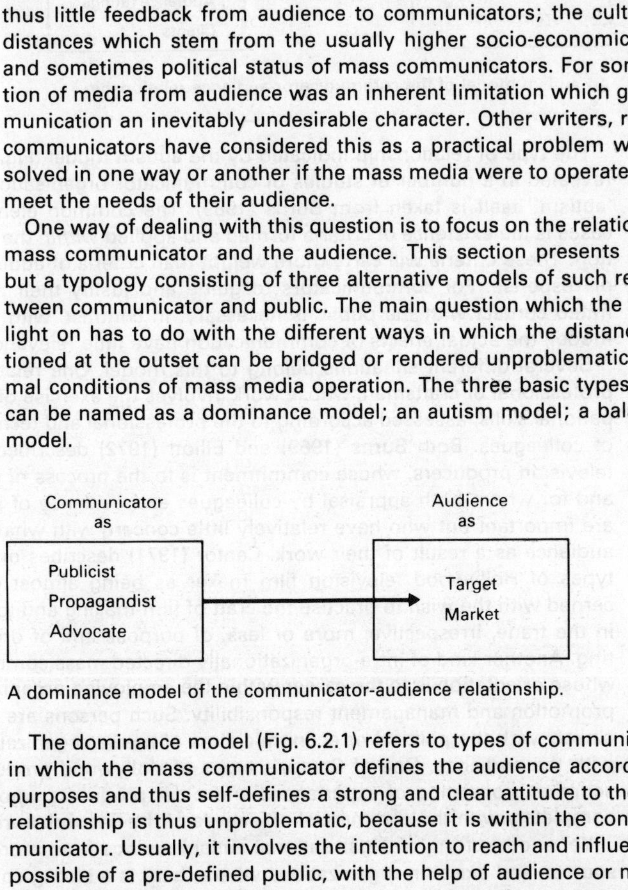

Fig. 6.2.1 A dominance model of the communicator-audience relationship.

The dominance model (Fig. 6.2.1) refers to types of communication situation in which the mass communicator defines the audience according to his own purposes and thus self-defines a strong and clear attitude to the audience. The relationship is thus unproblematic, because it is within the control of the communicator. Usually, it involves the intention to reach and influence as many as possible of a pre-defined public, with the help of audience or market research. The audience is a set of consumers or an object of mass persuasion. The case is exemplified by many advertising and political propaganda campaigns and could include public service as well as commercial campaigns, for instance those supporting health or safety practices, charitable appeals, etc. The label 'dominance' refers to the key feature of an intention to *impose* views and purposes of the sender on the receiver. Little fore knowledge or feedback is required, except some awareness of contact with the target audience and ultimately some indications of success or failure of the communicator's own purpose.

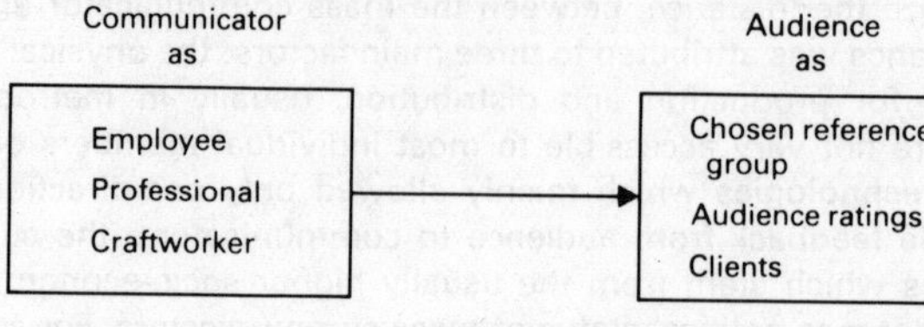

Fig. 6.2.2 An autism model of the communicator-audience relationship.

The type of relationship indicated by the autism model (Fig. 6.2.2.) has been revealed in a number of studies of communicator organisations and the term 'autism' itself is taken from Burns (1969). The common element in different cases is the existence of criteria formed and applied *within* the media organization. These criteria will carry more weight than criteria of audience satisfaction or response. For communicators to guide and justify their activities only limited contact with the public is necessary. In contrast, with the 'dominance' model, the actual *effects* of communication have little relevance.

Several different situations belong to this model. One relates to the media professional or craftsman, whose work involves the exercise of particular occupational skills, assessed according to the professional and technical judgement of colleagues. Both Burns (1969) and Elliott (1972) described the attitude of television producers, whose commitment is to the process of production itself and for whom both appraisal by colleagues and evidence of audience ratings are important but who have relatively little concern with what happens *to* the audience as a result of their work. Cantor (1971) describes one of three main types of Hollywood television film maker as being almost exclusively concerned with the wish to practise the craft of film-making and to get established in the trade, irrespective, more or less, of purpose and of organizational setting. Another kind of intra-organizationally directed mass communicator is one whose orientation is to the career within the employing organization, aiming at promotion and management responsibility. Such persons are likely to identify closely with the political or economic aims of media organizations rather than with the audience. One of Cantor's types of Hollywood producer fits this description, consisting of experienced and older producers who identify almost completely with the commercial objectives of the network bureaucracies.

Yet another form of organizational autism springs from more highprincipled sources and exists in organizations where there is a strong corporate philosophy or traditional defining the social role of the organization and thus also a relationship to the audience which is of a paternalist or sacerdotal kind. Burns (1969) suggests that the BBC offers this sort of role definition to its staff and a similar phenomenon is likely to occur in long established élite newspapers such as *The Times*.

Finally, in connection with this model of 'media-public relationships' we can mention the importance of an orientation to sources to be described more fully in the following section. Tunstall's work on journalists (1971) documents the existence of specialized journalist functions (such as foreign correspondent or parliamentary lobby correspondent) where the public as a whole is much less important than either a limited élite audience or a set of potential sources who are also part of this special public. The types of occupational outlook which are included under the heading of 'autism' are very different, but all involve a relatively low degree of direct orientation to the general public.

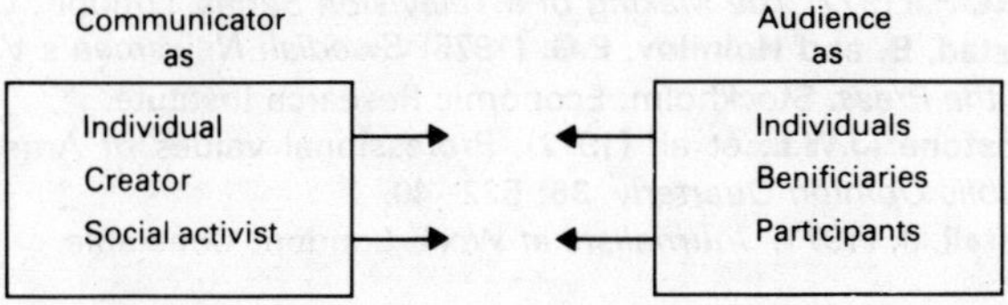

Fig. 6.2.3 A balance/exchange model of the communicator-audience relationship

The situation represented by Fig. 6.2.3 relates to the case where a communicator seeks to make contact with his audience on the basis of knowledge and response. There is no manipulative purpose, no corporate or collective organizational goal but a wish by an individual to connect with others. The model implies a willingness to respond to the needs, interests and reactions of the audience, to carry over into mass communication the kind of relationships which are more likely to hold in non-mass communication situations – like that of playwright and actor to public, speaker to audience, author to small selective readership. Or it could represent circumstances of local or community based communication where senders and receivers share the same culture, environment, problems and aspirations. The type stands for a recognizable communication ideal, although documented examples from research are not so common. Even so, Cantor (1971) names one type of Hollywood TV producer as someone who is committed to the craft of writing, who wants to film stories with messages which have some meaning and value to the public, who values independence and artistic autonomy. There are many individual writers, performers, producers who see the mass media as a vehicle for sharing a personal vision or experience with a large public. Several studies of journalistic roles (e.g. Fjaestad and Holmlov 1975; Johnstone et al. 1972) identify a role attributed by journalists themselves to the press as active participant in social and political processes.

The differences between the three models may be summarized in terms of different kinds of reward experienced by the main communicator. In the dominance model the source of reward is usually external to the communication activity – the achievement of some other objective. In the second case the reward comes from the immediate working environment – the practice of professional skills. In the third case reward comes from the relationships established through communication with a wider like-minded public.

Comment This is only one way of looking at a very complex problem and instances of communication are unlikely to fit one single type.

References

Burns, T. (1969) 'Public service and private world' in P. Halmos (ed.), *The Sociology of Mass Media Communicators.* Sociology Review Monographs, no. 13.

Cantor, M. (1971) *The Hollywood Television Producer.* New York: Basic Books.

Elliott, P. (1972) *The Making of a Television Series.* London: Constable.

Fjaestad, B. and **Holmlov, P.G.** (1975) *Swedish Newsmen's Views on the Role of the Press.* Stockholm, Economic Research Institute.

Johnstone, J.W.L. et al. (1972) 'Professional values of American newsmen', *Public Opinion Quarterly*, **36**: 522–40.

Tunstall, J. (1971) *Journalists at Work.* London: Constable.

6.3 GIEBER AND JOHNSON'S MODEL OF SOURCE-REPORTER RELATIONSHIPS

The authors of a study of reporter and source roles, Gieber and Johnson (1961), made use of some basic elements in the Westley and MacLean model (2.5) to illustrate some alternative possibilities in the relationship between reporters and sources, at least at the local community level.

The model can be presented in three parts, Figs. 6.3.1, 6.3.2 and 6.3.3, each standing for one of the possibilities in the structure of the relationship. In each case, the symbol A is the source and corresponds to the A or 'advocate' in the model of Westley and MacLean, from which this model in part derives. The symbol C is the communicator role, in this case the reporter assigned to the 'City Hall beat'. The model derives from empirical research into the way the reporter covers news of local politics.

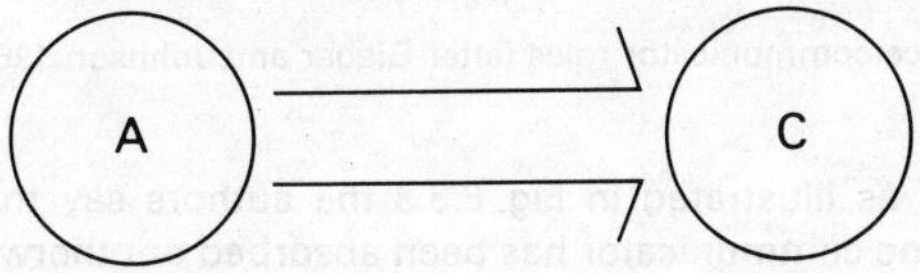

Fig. 6.3.1 Separate source-communicator roles (after Gieber and Johnson 1961).

The relationship shown in Fig. 6.3.1 is described as follows by the authors: 'The communication acts of the two communicators, A and C, respectively, take place within frames of reference (the circles) separated by well differentiated bureaucratic functions, role assignments and perceptions, social distance, values, etc. The flow of information in channels (double line) tends to be formal.'

This model represents the classic case of a free press, in that there is assumed to be a complete independence between the social systems involved, the one 'making news', the other objectively reporting what happens. This case can apply in circumstances of distance and infrequency of contact between source and journalist.

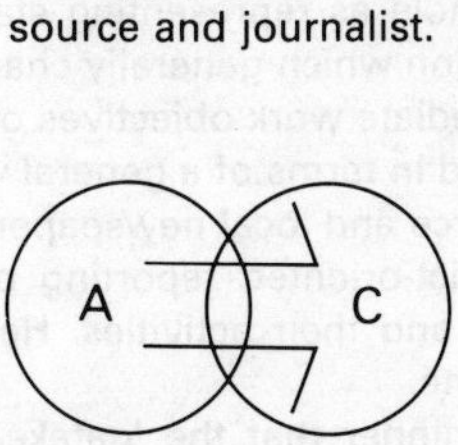

Fig. 6.3.2 Partially assimilated source and communicator roles (after Gieber and Johnson 1961).

The relationship in Fig. 6.3.2 can be expressed as follows: The frames of reference of A and C overlap; the two communicators co-operate in achieving their communication roles and, in part, share the values underlying the communication roles and acts.

This version of the relationship is closer to what seems to happen in practice in such a relationship. The participants co-operate with each other and form a mutually agreed perception of their function. They have certain objectives in common, the one needing to get a particular story into a newspaper, the other needing to get news to satisfy his editor. The implication is that there will be some loss of independence by the C role, who should be acting as impartial agent of the public 'need to know'.

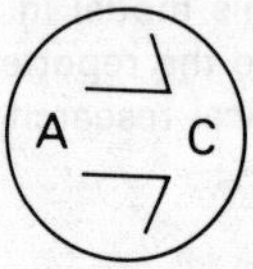

Fig. 6.3.3 Assimilated source-communicator roles (after Gieber and Johnson 1961).

Of the version as illustrated in Fig. 6.3.3 the authors say that 'The frame of reference for one communicator has been absorbed or otherwise taken over by the other; there is no distinction in role performance and values'. In principle, the model can accommodate a process of assimilation in either direction. It would be conceivable that a public official could supply information solely according to the demands and interests of the press. In reality, the pressure towards assimilation is nearly always in the other direction, since the supplier of information usually is in a stronger position in the relationship. The giving or withholding of news is a more effective sanction in day-to-day affairs than the longer-term sanction of inadequate or unfavourable publicity. The research example on which the model is based supports such an interpretation. Assimilation also occurs when the goals of the press are identified with the goals of the society, as in many socialist societies, or in circumstances of totalitarian or autocratic control.

Comment The models should be taken as a whole as representing stages along a continuum of collaboration and assimilation which generally characterizes sources and news reporters. Apart from immediate work objectives of the reporter, the tendency to co-operate can be justified in terms of a general value of the 'good of the community' to which both source and local newspaper are likely to subscribe. Such a value penalizes conflict-oriented reporting or the retailing of 'negative' news about local officials and their activities. Hence collaboration does not derive from self-interest alone.

The model serves as a useful reminder that the 'gatekeeper' is part of a wider system of social relations and normative controls. It also captures the important fact that news does not simply flow into the impartial arms of the gatekeeper (as studies of telegraph editing seem to suggest). Rather, it is in some measure sought out and constructed in a bargaining relationship in which the work interests of participants and some of the goals of the original source and interests of ultimate readers play a part. Recent research on British media has given a good deal of support to the intermediate version of this relationship, as shown in Fig. 6.3.2 (e.g. Chibnall 1975; Murphy 1974).

References

Chibnall, S. (1975) *Law and Order News*. London: Constable.

Gieber, W. and **Johnson, W.** (1961) 'The City Hall beat: a study of reporter and source roles', *Journalism Quarterly*, **38**: 289–97.

Murphy, D. (1974) *The Silent Watchdog*. London: Constable.

6.4 WHITE'S GATEKEEPER MODEL

The concept of *gatekeeper* has been frequently used in studies of the mass communication process, especially, but not solely, with reference to any action within a media organization which involved choosing or rejecting some potential item for publication.

The concept originated in work carried out by Kurt Lewin (1947) dealing with decisions about household food purchases. He noted that information has always to flow along certain channels which contain 'gate areas', where decisions are made, either according to impartial rules or personally by 'gatekeeper', as to whether information or goods will be allowed to enter in, or continue, in the channel. In a side reference, he invoked a comparison with the flow of news in mass communication. This idea was taken up and applied by White (1950) in a study of the telegraph wire editor of an American non-metropolitan paper, whose decision to discard many items was seen as the most significant gatekeeping activity. The model underlying this study can be expressed as in Fig. 6.4.1.

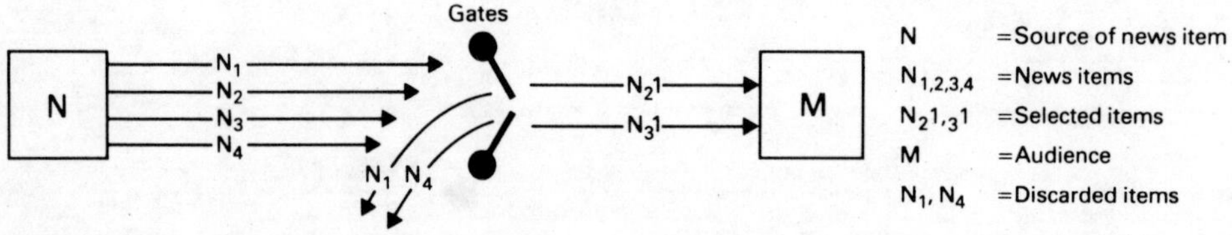

Fig. 6.4.1 White's simple gatekeeping model (after White 1950).

This model has been extended and criticized in later work, although it has served as the basis for subsequent research into the process of selection from news agency copy. Chronologically, it was succeeded by the Westley and MacLean model (described above) which is also, amongst other things, a gatekeeper model and which tends to emphasize the system context in which gatekeeping takes place.

Comment Apart from its obvious simplicity, there are a number of weaknesses in this original White model which have led to its modification or, for some purposes, replacement. Firstly, the model takes no account of organizational factors which constrain and direct the process and it lends itself to rather personalized interpretations of the activity being studied. Secondly, the model suggests there is only *one* main 'gate area'. Thirdly, the model implies a rather passive activity as far as the flow of news is concerned. There is an impression from the model, that there is a continuous and free flow of a wide range of news which has only to be tapped in ways which suit a particular newspaper. In spite

of these criticisms, this conceptualization has been extremely influential in matters beyond the scope of the original research and White contributed a name to a whole school of research on communicators.

References

Lewin, K. (1947) 'Channels of group life', *Human Relations*, **1**: 143–53.
White, D.M. (1950) 'The "Gatekeepers": a case study in the selection of news', *Journalism Quarterly*, **27**: 383–90.

6.5 MCNELLY'S MODEL OF NEWS FLOW

An early point of criticism of the White model was that it showed only one gatekeeper rather than several, as one would normally expect to find in a complex news operation. McNelly's model (1959) is addressed to this particular problem, since it seeks to represent the various intermediary communicators standing between the event and the ultimate receiver (newspaper, reader, etc.).

The process which the model represents can be described in the following way, taking a hypothetical foreign news event. A foreign news agency correspondent learns of a newsworthy event and writes a report which goes first to a regional bureau, from where it may be sent in shortened form to the agency central bureau. There, it may be combined with a related story from elsewhere and sent to a national or regional bureau of the country, where it may be again cut for transmission to the telegraph editor of a newspaper or radio/television

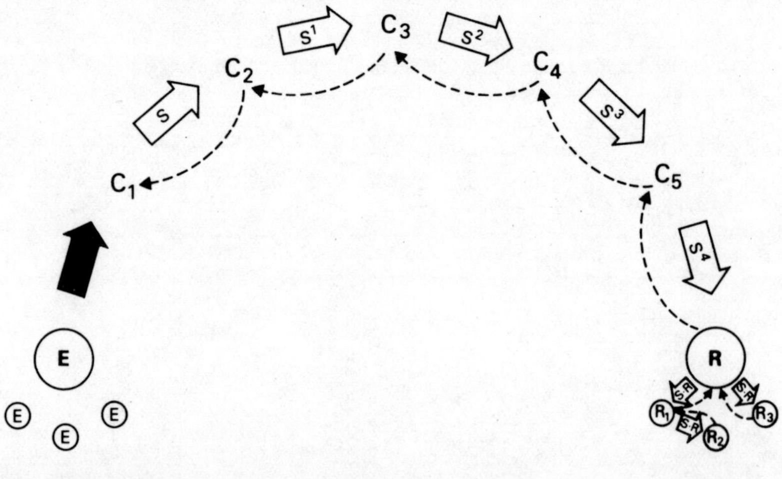

Fig. 6.5.1 McNelly's model of intermediary communicators in news flow, showing news passing different 'gatekeepers' (after McNelly 1959).

Key to symbols in diagram:
E = Newsworthy event
C_1 = Foreign agency correspondent
C_2 = Regional bureau editor
C_3 = Agency central bureau editor or deskman
C_4 = National or regional home bureau editor
C_5 = Telegraph editor or radio or TV news editor
S, S^1, S^3, etc. = The report in a succession of altered (shortened) forms
R = Receiver
R_1, R_2, etc. = Family members, friends, associates, etc.
S – R = Story as modified by word of mouth transmission
Dotted line = feedback

station. Here it is further cut before it reaches the reader or listener. Further selection then occurs and the story may either be ignored or alternatively passed on by word of mouth to a succession of people. Throughout the process, various forms of feedback response occur which may guide further acts of transmission (see Fig. 6.5.1)

Comment The important points emphasized by the model are:

1. the fact that the most important gatekeeping may well have been completed before the news reaches the telegraph editor of a newspaper, especially in the case of foreign news where global news decisions are made in the major bureaux of big telegraph services;
2. gatekeeping is much more than just selecting or rejecting, since the intermediaries often alter the form and substance of those stories that survive the journey;
3. gatekeeping does not end with the news medium, since the initial receiver often acts as gatekeeper for others;
4. feedback (broken lines in the diagram) is often infrequent and delayed.

The model is still in some respects incomplete in its own terms, since it could be extended at its initial stages. It tends to take 'newsworthiness' for granted and treats the agency correspondent as the primary source. There may well be two or three additional stages: there will be a witness to an event or one of the participants, thence often a local report, taken up by a stringer, and passed to the agency correspondent.

Reference

McNelly, J.T. (1959) 'Intermediary communicators in the international flow of news', *Journalism Quarterly*, **36**: 23–6.

6.6 BASS' 'DOUBLE ACTION MODEL' OF INTERNAL NEWS FLOW

Bass (1969) in a revision of the gatekeeper theory suggests a simple but important elaboration of existing models. His main criticism of previous conceptualizations in both White and McNelly is that there is no differentiation between the roles of different 'gatekeepers' and no indication of what is the most significant point of selection. He argues that the most important gatekeeping activity occurs within the news organization and that the process should be divided into two stages, that of *newsgathering* and news *processing*, as shown in Fig. 6.6.1.

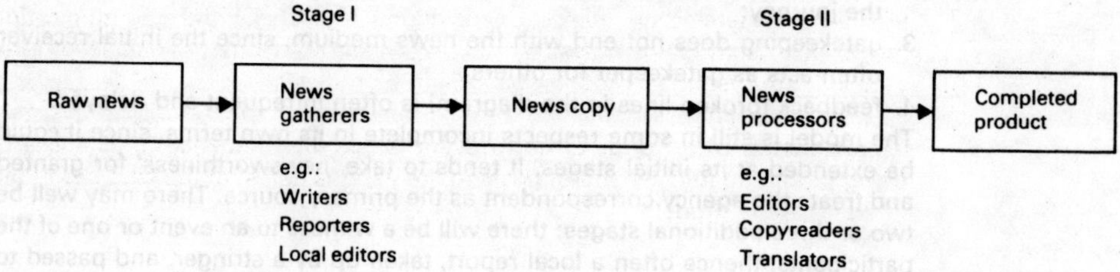

Fig. 6.6.1 Newsgathering and news processing are separate aspects of news production (after Bass 1969).

The first step occurs when the newsgatherers make 'raw news' – events, speeches and news conferences – into 'news copy' or news items. The second step occurs when the news processors modify and unify the items into the 'completed product' – a newspaper or a news broadcast – that is delivered to the public.

Comment

This model has been found useful in studies of journalistic activity (e.g. Tunstall 1972) and the two-fold division helps to separate those who are likely to be closest to sources and most oriented to them from those who are acting more literally in the gatekeeping sense by choosing, changing or excluding an incoming flow of content.

References

Bass, A.Z. (1969) 'Refining the gatekeeper concept', *Journalism Quarterly*, **46**: 69–71.

Tunstall, J.T. (1972) *Journalists at Work*. London: Constable.

6.7 GALTUNG AND RUGE'S MODEL OF SELECTIVE GATEKEEPING

The model to be described here is not strictly an advance on, or development of, those gatekeeping models which have already been discussed. It rests on a relatively simple version of the flow of news and of gatekeeping as a process of successive selections according to a number of news values or criteria which affect the perception of news events.

For us, its main interest is that it develops in some detail one aspect of gatekeeping which is neglected or dealt with only in general terms by other models, namely the criteria which are applied in deciding whether to select or reject. If these criteria are completely subjective and vary from one gatekeeper to another, there is no point in considering them from the communication model perspective. However, there is reason to believe that the selection process is fairly systematic and in some degree predictable.

Galtung and Ruge approach the problem by naming and describing the main characteristics of an original news event which will influence its chances of being picked up initially and of passing the various gates, of the kind described in the McNelly model.

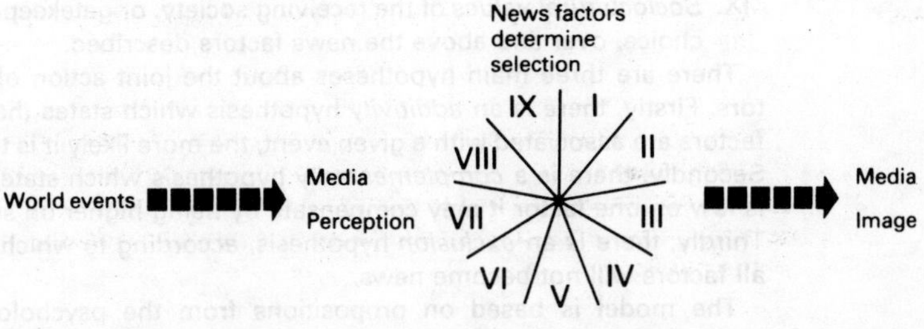

Fig. 6.7.1 Galtung and Ruge specify news factors which intervene between event and media image.

The model in Fig. 6.7.1 represents the process by which world events are converted by media organizations into a 'media image' or picture of the world which is distributed to the audience. The application of the model to problems of explanation and prediction depends on a few basic hypotheses about the way in which these variables or 'news factors' alone or in combination affect selection and rejection.

The news factors are, briefly, as follows:

I. *Timespan.* An event is more likely to be noticed if its occurrence fits the time schedule of the medium concerned. For instance, an event begun and completed in a few hours or less suits a daily newspaper or a news broadcast while a complex event taking several days to develop suits a weekly newspaper. Some events are too slow in developing, however important, to be really 'newsworthy' for the mass media.

II. *Intensity or threshold value.* An event is more likely to be noticed if it is of great magnitude, or if its normal level of significance suddenly increases so as to attract particular notice. The latter applies where there is normally some surveillance by the media, e.g. of government or financial matters, or an ongoing conflict.

III. *Clarity/lack of ambiguity.* The less the meaning of an event is in doubt, the more likely it is to be suitable for news treatment.

IV. *Cultural proximity or relevance.* The closer the event to the culture and interests of the intended audience, the more likely is selection.

V. *Consonance.* An event which conforms to certain established expectations or preconceptions is more likely to be selected than one which does not conform to expectations. For instance, there are parts of the world where conflict is expected, some activities are inherently dangerous, others are associated with political change, etc.

VI. *Unexpectedness.* Amongst events which are equally consonant in the sense of V, the more unusual and unpredictable the actual event, the more likely it is to be selected.

VII. *Continuity.* Once an event has been defined as newsworthy, there will be some momentum to the continued noticing of the event or related happenings.

VIII. *Composition.* News events are selected according to their place in a balanced whole (newspaper or newscast) and some events are consequently selected on grounds of contrast.

IX. *Sociocultural values* of the receiving society, or gatekeepers, will influence choice, over and above the news factors described.

There are three main hypotheses about the joint action of these news factors. Firstly, there is an *additivity* hypothesis which states that the more news factors are associated with a given event, the more likely it is to become 'news'. Secondly, there is a *complementarity* hypothesis which states that if an event is low on one factor it may compensate by being higher on some other factor. Thirdly, there is an *exclusion* hypothesis, according to which an event low on all factors will not become news.

The model is based on propositions from the psychology of individual perception. It is an important implication of the model and one reason for its influence, that the outcome of gatekeeping along these lines is to produce an ordered structure or image of the places, people and events in the news and, moreover, one which differs significantly and predictably from 'reality'. It is important to stress that the model only applies to foreign news, although a similar version of the theory could be developed for domestic news.

Comment

The approach described has been extremely influential in studies of news content and some confirmation is claimed on the basis of empirical testing (Galtung and Ruge 1965; Smith 1969; Sande 1971).

Rosengren (1974) mentions three main grounds of criticism. Firstly, it is too psychological, and depends too much on ideas about selective perception by individual gatekeepers. He recommends an alternative approach which takes more account of political and economic factors governing news reporting. In short, the set of news factors can be incomplete, without noting the particular circumstances of the political and economic relations between the countries concerned.

Secondly, Rosengren argues that the model is untestable and not open to falsification, because, taken together, the additivity and complementarity hypotheses can apply to all cases.

Thirdly, the model has not yet been adequately tested with an appropriate methodology. A satisfactory test would require reference to 'extra-media' data – evidence of other (e.g. political/economic) variables and also independent sources of knowledge about the 'reality' of events which were, or were not, covered. These criticisms leave open the possibility of an improvement in the explanatory power of the model by adding new variables and extending the methodology. A recent application of the scheme to the analysis of news on Dutch television (Bergsma 1978) has cast some doubt on the general tenability of the complementarity hypothesis, but has shown the utility of the scheme in studying the operation of news values.

References

Bergsma, F. (1978), 'News values in foreign affairs on Dutch television', *Gazette*, **24**: 207–22.

Galtung, J. and **Ruge, M.H.** (1965) 'The structure of foreign news', *Journal of Peace Research*, **2**: 64–90.

Rosengren, K.E. (1974) 'International news: methods, data, theory', *Journal of Peace Research*, **11**: 145–56.

Sande, O. (1971) 'The perception of foreign news', *Journal of Peace Research*, **8**: 223–37.

Smith, R.F. (1969) 'On the structure of foreign news: a comparison of the *New York Times* and the Indian White Papers', *Journal of Peace Research*, **6**: 23–6.

INDEX